CUTEST EVER
BABY TOYS

CUTEST EVER
BABY TOYS

30 ADORABLE PROJECTS
TO KNIT AND CROCHET

Val Pierce

NH
NEW
HOLLAND

First published in 2014 by
New Holland Publishers
London • Sydney • Cape Town • Auckland
www.newhollandpublishers.com • www.newholland.com.au

The Chandlery Unit 114 50 Westminster Bridge Road London SE1 7QY
1/66 Gibbes Street Chatswood NSW 2067 Australia
Wembley Square First Floor Solan Road Gardens Cape Town 8001 South Africa
218 Lake Road Northcote Auckland New Zealand

A catalogue record of this book is available at the British Library and at the National Library of Australia

ISBN: 9781742574165

10 9 8 7 6 5 4 3 2 1

Publisher: Fiona Schultz
Editor: Simona Hill
Designer: Tracy Loughlin
Stylist: Sue Stubbs
Photographer: Sue Stubbs
Production director: Olga Dementiev
Printer: Toppan Leefung Printing Limited

Follow New Holland Publishers on
Facebook: www.facebook.com/NewHollandPublishers

Contents

Introduction

Everyone loves making toys for newborn babies and little people. These items are usually cute, bright and colourful and being small in scale, are generally quick to make. With all these requirements in mind I have designed 30 gifts and toys for you to make that are sure to delight the recipient as much as the project maker. From a cuddly penguin to a brightly coloured play ball, a lovely friendly dinosaur to some sweet little bootees, you are sure to find something in this volume to make for that special little person.

You will see that most toy patterns are usually knitted in either garter stitch or stocking stitch using smaller needles than would normally be used for the weight of yarn. The reason for this is so that the resulting fabric will be of a more dense texture, be firmer to the touch and will not stretch too much when stuffed, and the stuffing shouldn't migrate through the fabric.

CHOOSING DESIGNS AND YARNS

Before you begin, it is very important to bear in mind the age of the child that you are making the project for. Babies and toddlers will constantly put things into their mouths to investigate them. These toys will need to be washed quite frequently so it's sensible to buy good quality wool that is machine washable.

The younger the child, the more basic and simple the toy needs to be. Bright bold colours, different textures and easy-to-hold shapes are perfect for tiny babies. The older the child then the more elaborate you can make the project.

When you have chosen the design you want to make, decide which yarn you might like to use. The choice these days is so varied that it can be quite a task to choose, though often an enjoyable one. Although I have stated yarn weights for each project and specified the yarns I used to make these items it is possible to make almost every toy from oddments of the correct weight yarn from your stash.

Additionally the suggested yarn might not be available from your local wool store, or you may have yarn that you wish to use. Again, keep in mind the age of the child. Eyelash yarns and yarns with metallic threads running through them are fine for older children but the fibres may shed a little and therefore I would recommend testing them before using them to make gifts for babies.

TIPS FOR SEWING UP YOUR PROJECT

Having spent many hours knitting all the components needed to make the project, you will need to sew the pieces together. Take as much care sewing up the pieces as you would when making a garment, that way, arms and legs will be the same size, and the whole toy will be in proportion when it's finished. It is always better to count rows and fit like to like, so when you sew them together all the rows will match.

Fabrics can be stitched together using more than one method. Garter stitch is much neater sewn on the right sides of the fabric. Arranging the pieces flat and side by side, you can match row for row by sewing through the 'little bumps' of the garter stitch alternately, then pulling the yarn quite firmly to draw the pieces together. This gives a neat, flat and almost invisible join. You will find it much easier to see what you are doing when the right sides of the fabric are facing you too. You can also join stocking stitch in a similar way, but this time sewing through between the 'V' made by a stitch and picking up the horizontal loop in the centre of it. You will work picking up the stitch alternately on adjacent sides of the fabric, then drawing the work together quite tightly. This gives an invisible seam and allows you to match stripes and patterns really easily. A third method used is back stitch. This is worked on the inside of the fabric, and gives a small neat ridge, it is more bulky than the other two methods of seaming but it can be very strong so is a good option when you need strength adding to a particular join.

TIPS FOR STUFFING YOUR PROJECT

Novice toy makers are often quite nervous about stuffing their toys fearing that they may spoil them. Most toy parts will need to be stuffed quite firmly so that they hold their shape. Do this by adding a small amount of stuffing at a time and pushing it well into the base of the part you are working on. I always tease out each piece as I use it, that way it is more pliable and more likely to achieve a smooth shape. Always try to stuff each part equally, so check legs and arms against each other as you work to make sure that they match. Don't over-stuff pieces since you need to be able to sew limbs to the body and if they are full to the brim then there will be no spare fabric to use. Hands and feet will need extra stuffing and shaping.

Heads need to be shaped to give the best possible result. Look at the photograph as you work to check the shape and see where extra stuffing may be needed. Take care and work slowly. Check frequently that the head isn't becoming too big for the body and vice versa. The toy needs to be stable and not top heavy. You can shape and stuff as you work, pushing more into some areas such as cheeks and noses and less into others. Don't sew on any facial features until you are satisfied with the shape of the head. Loosely tack (baste) the head to the body to see how it sits in proportion to the rest of the toy. You can always take out or add more stuffing at this stage. Only when you are completely satisfied should you sew the head to the body. To avoid a wobbly head, a result of the head and body not being equally stuffed, add a little more stuffing or remove a little by opening a tiny part of a

seam. First catch the head to the body with a few stitches around the neck. This will hold it steady while you sew the two pieces more firmly together. Check all the time that the head is straight, not too far back or too far forward. Mostly heads face forward and are straight. Angling the head very slightly can add a cute look.

Before stitching the arms and legs to a toy check that they are stuffed equally and that the shaping matches. Pin the limbs into position before you sew them in place. Try to get equal distances between the pieces and check whether your toy needs to be sitting or standing.

Using matching yarn and a blunt-ended needle, use any long tail ends from the casting on or off, for sewing up the pieces. Sew the limbs onto the body very firmly, taking a stitch on the limb and then a stitch on the body alternately until you have sewn it firmly in place. Go over the same area twice if you are unsure whether the stitching is firm enough.

ADDING FACIAL AND OTHER FEATURES

Adding features is the *piece de resistance* and can make or break the success of the look of your toy. It takes practice to get features looking just right so try out your techniques on a spare piece of fabric before you begin. Look at the photograph of the face you are going to copy. Note the placement of the eyes and nose and mouth. Put markers on the face in the areas where those features will go before you begin. Safety eyes need to be added when the head is partially stuffed. Once they are locked in place you can't remove and reposition them. Push the eye through the fabric in the desired position, then push the washer onto the back of the eye, it will 'click' when it is correctly placed. When embroidering features you can, of course, unpick and re-embroider them, if needed.

There are many ways of adding embroidered features. Most noses for larger animals can be stitched with straight stitches placed quite close together so that they form a dense mass. Using wool or embroidery thread and a blunt-ended nee-dle, work consecutive lines in close parallel to each other. It is easy to pull the yarn too tightly when doing this so work evenly and slowly to achieve a good result. Pulling too tightly will result in a puckered piece of fabric and an odd-shaped nose. Eyes can be embroidered using French knots. If you keep the tension even for each eye, you can add shape to the face. Their positon can also help to depict the nose too. Prac-tice is the only way to achieve good results, but patience is needed too. So, if you get it wrong first time, then unpick and start again. You will be glad you did when you see your finished toy.

KNITTING ABBREVIATIONS

Alt = alternate
Beg = beginning
Cm =centimetres
Foll = following
Garter stitch = every row knit
Inc = increase
K = knit
P = purl
Patt = pattern
Psso = pass slipped stitch over
Rem = remain
rep = repeat
RS = right side
Skpso = sl 1, K1, pass slipped stitch over
St = stitch
Stocking Stitch = alternating knit and purl rows
WS = wrong side
Yfwd = yarn forward over needle to make a hole

CROCHET ABBREVIATIONS

Ch = chain
Dc = double crochet (US: single crochet)
Dc2tog = work the next 2dc together to decrease a stitch
Htr = half treble
Sl st = slipped stitch
Tr = treble (US: double crochet)

UK AND US TERMINOLOGY

Cast off	=	Bind off
Moss stitch	=	Seed stitch
Stocking stitch	=	Stockinette stitch
Yarn forward	=	Yarn over

KNITTING NEEDLE CONVERSION CHART

Metric	UK	US
2 mm	14	0
2.25 mm	13	1
2.75 mm	12	2
3 mm	11	–
3.25 mm	10	3
3.5 mm	–	4
3.75 mm	9	5
4 mm	8	6
4.5 mm	7	7
5 mm	6	8
5.5 mm	5	9
6 mm	4	10

CROCHET HOOK CONVERSION CHART

Metric	US	UK
2 mm	–	14
2.25	B/1	13
2.5	–	12
2.75	C/2	–
3	–	11
3.25	D/3	10
35	E/4	9
3.75	F/5	–
4	G/6	8
4.5	7	7
5	H/8	6
5.5	I/9	5
6	J/10	4

Great Big Dinosaur

Little boys and girls will love this dinosaur buddy. He is easy to carry around with his long neck and is just waiting for hugs. Making the toy will take time and patience but is well worth the effort. I have used felt to make the eyes, but you can easily embroider them, if you prefer.

✹✹✹ Experienced

YOU WILL NEED
2 x 50 g (2 oz) balls Patons Fairytale
   Dreamtime DK random-dyed, shade
   4971 (A)
2 x 50 g (2 oz) balls Patons Fairytale
   Dreamtime DK lime green, shade 4952 (B)
1 x 50 g (2 oz) ball Patons Fairytale
   Dreamtime DK orange, shade 4951 (C)
Scraps of black and white felt, for the eyes
3.75 mm (UK 9, US 4) knitting needles
Safety toy stuffing
Wool needle, for sewing up
Sewing kit

TENSION
Is not critical on this project.

DINOSAUR
Using yarn A, cast on 16 sts.
Row 1: Purl.
Row 2: Inc knitwise into every stitch (32 sts).
Beg with a purl row, work 22 rows st st.
Row 25: (K2tog 6 times), inc in each of next 8 sts, (K2tog 6 times) (28 sts).
Inc 1 st at each end of next and every foll 4th row until there are 38 sts.
Work 7 rows st st.
Next row: Inc knitwise in each st to end (76 sts).
Work 30 rows st st.
Next row: (K2, K2tog) to end.
Work 14 rows st st.
Next row: (K1, K2tog) to end.
Work 9 rows st st.

Dec 1 st at each end of next and every alt row until 4 sts remain. Cast off. This is the tail end.

Spots
Make 8
Using yarn C, cast on 3 sts.
Row 1: Knit.
Row 2: Inc in first and last stitch.
Knit 3 rows.
Dec 1 st at each end of next row.
Row 7: Knit.
Row 8: Sl 1, K2tog, psso. Fasten off.

Back Plates
Make 8
Using yarn B, cast on 2 sts.
Row 1: Knit.
Row 2: Inc in each st (4 sts).
Row 3: Knit.
Row 4: Inc in first stitch, knit to last st, inc.
Cont as for rows 3 and 4 until there are 12 sts on the needle. Slip the sts onto a spare needle. Make 7 more plates in the same way. Now work across all the plates, slipping each off the spare needle and onto the knitting needle as you do (96 sts).
Knit 2 rows. Cast off.

Legs
Make 4
Using yarn A, cast on 18 sts.
Row 1: Purl.
Row 2: Inc knitwise into each stitch to end of row (36 sts).
Work 8 rows st st on these rows.

Row 11: K8, (K2tog 10 times), K8 (26 sts).
Work 13 rows st st beg with a purl row.
Row 25: K6, (K2tog 3 times), K2, (K2tog 3 times), K6.
Row 26: Purl.
Cast off.

ASSEMBLING THE DINOSAUR
Sew in all loose ends. Fold in half, right sides together so that the body seam runs underneath the dinosaur. Stitch seam firmly leaving the head and tail ends open for stuffing. Turn right sides out and stuff the shape, working from each end, adding a little at a time, and pushing the stuffing into place with the blunt end of the knitting needle. Work slowly and fill firmly. When you are happy with the shape, secure the nose and tail openings.

Cut shapes from felt for the eyes and sew in place on the head, or embroider them, if your prefer.

Embroider the nostrils and smiley mouth with black yarn. Sew the spots on in a random pattern.

Pin the plates in place along the back of the dinosaur, sew firmly on each side to make them stand up.

Sew up the leg seams leaving the tops open, and stuff firmly. Attach the legs to the dinosaur making sure they are level so that he will stand on a flat surface.

Halloween Bootees

These super-cute little orange bootees will be so fun for baby to wear on Halloween, though you could change the colours to suit your own special occasion. Use all one shade of yarn or mix and match whatever colours you have in your stash.

❋ Beginner

YOU WILL NEED
1 x 50 g (2 oz) ball Patons Fairytale
  Dreamtime DK orange, shade 4951
1 x 50 g (2 oz) ball Patons Fairytale
  Dreamtime DK green, shade 4952
1 m (1 yd) narrow matching green ribbon
2 orange flower buttons
4 mm (UK 8, US 6) knitting needles
Wool needle, for sewing up
Sewing kit

SIZE
To fit baby 3–6 months

TENSION
22 sts x 30 rows st st measure 10 cm (4 in) using 4 mm needles.

SPECIAL ABBREVIATIONS
M1 = Make 1 stitch by picking up the strand between the stitch you have just knitted and the next stitch on the needle, then knitting into the back of it.

BOOTEES

Make 2
Using orange yarn, cast on 27 sts.
Knit 1 row.
Row 2: K2 (M1, K11, M1, K1) twice, K1 (31 sts).
Row 3 and following alternate rows: Knit.
Row 5: K2, M1, K12, M1, K3, M1, K12, M1, K2
(35 sts).
Row 7: K2, M1, K13, M1, K5, M1, K13, M1, K2
(39 sts).
Row 9: K2, M1, K14, M1, K7, M1, K14, M1, K2
(43 sts).
Change to green yarn and work 6 rows st
st. Break yarn. (These 6 rows will be folded
in half and sewn together to form the ridge
around the base of the bootee.)
Join in orange and work 12 rows garter st.
Shape instep
Next row: K26, turn.
Next row: K9, turn.
Next row: K8, K2tog, turn.
Next row: K8, K2togtbl, turn.
Rep last two rows 5 times more, turn.
Next row: K9, knit across rem sts on the
left-hand needle.
Next row: Knit across all sts (31 sts).
Work 2 rows in garter st.
Make eyelets: K2, *yfwd, k2tog, K1*, rep from
* to * to last 2 sts, yfwd, K2tog.
Next row: Knit.
Change to green yarn.
Knit 4 rows.
Next row: Purl.
Next row: Knit.
Next row: Knit.
Next row: Purl.

Next row: Knit.
Next row: Knit.
Next row: Purl.
Next row: Knit.
Next row: Knit.
Next row: Purl. Break off green yarn.
Join orange yarn and knit 4 rows. Cast off.

ASSEMBLING THE BOOTEES

Fold the six green rows of st st in half
onto the right side of the work. Working
from the wrong side of the bootee, catch
the corresponding stitches from the top
and bottom of the rows to hold the ridge
together. Sew the foot and back seams on
the bootees.

Cut the ribbon in half and thread a piece
through the eyelet holes on each bootee
and tie in a bow. Sew a button to the front of
each bootee.

Tilly the Tortoise

Who can resist this cute little crocheted tortoise with her flowers and frilly shell?

Inside she has a bell rattle that is sure to captivate the interest of little people. With

her bright colours and adorable face she will soon become a treasured toy.

❄❄ Intermediate

YOU WILL NEED

1 x 50 g (2 oz) ball Patons Fairytale
  Dreamtime DK lime, shade 04952
1 x 50 g (2 oz) ball Patons Fairytale
  Dreamtime DK lemon, shade 04960
Oddments of DK in turquoise, orange, pink,
  green, yellow, pale blue, cream
Black yarn, for the features
4 mm (UK 8, US G 8) crochet hook
Toy safety stuffing
Bell safety rattle insert
Wool needle, for sewing up
Sewing kit

SIZE

22 cm (8½ in) from head to tail
11 cm (4¼ in) standing height

TENSION

Is not critical on this project.

Next round: 1ch, *1dc into each of next 3dc, 2dc into next dc*, rep to end, join as before. Cont to increase in this manner until you reach the row 1dc into each of next 7dc, 2dc into next dc*. ****

Next round: 1ch, work 1dc into each dc to end, join with a sl st.

Repeat last round 9 more times.

Break lime and join in turquoise.

Next round: 3ch, work 2tr into each dc all around, join with a sl st.

Break turquoise and join in orange.

Do not turn but work 1dc into each tr, working from right to left to form a corded edge.

BASE

Using lemon, work as body to ****, fasten off.

LEGS

Make 4

Using lemon, make 3ch, work 11tr into third ch from hook. Join into a ring with a sl st.

Next round: 3ch, work 2tr into each tr to end, join as before and fasten off.

HEAD

Using lime, make 2 ch.

Work 6dc into second ch from hook. Join into a circle with a sl st.

Round 1: 1ch, work 2dc into each dc to end, join with sl st (12dc).

Round 2: 1ch, *1dc into next dc, 2dc into next dc*, rep from * to * to end, join as before (18dc).

Round 3: 1ch, *1dc into each of next 2dc, 2dc

TORTOISE

BODY

Using lime, make 2 ch.

Work 6dc into second ch from hook. Join into a circle with a sl st.

Next round: 1ch, work 2dc into each dc to end, join with sl st (12dc).

Next round: 1ch, *1dc into next dc, 2dc into next dc*, rep to end, join as before (18dc).

Next round: 1ch, *1dc into each of next 2dc, 2dc into next dc*, rep to end, join as before (24dc).

into next dc*, rep from * to * to end, join as before (24dc).

Round 4: 1 ch, 1dc into each dc to end, join with a sl st.

Rep last round twice more.

Round 7: 1ch, *1dc into each of next 2dc, dc2tog*, rep from * to * to end, join with a sl st.

Round 8: 1ch, *1dc into next dc, dc2tog*, rep from * to * to end, join with a sl st. Fasten off.

TAIL

Using lime, make 10dc. Join into a ring.

Round 1: Work 1dc into each ch all around. Join with a sl st.

Repeat last round twice more.

Round 4: Dc2tog all around. Join as before.

Round 5: Work 1 round in dc. Join as before.

Round 6: Dc2tog twice, 1dc in last dc. Fasten off.

FLOWERS

Make 6 in various colours

Using colour of your choice, make 6ch. Join into a circle with a sl st.

Round 1: 1ch, work 8dc into a circle, join with a sl st. Join in next colour.

Round 2: *4ch, 1dc into next dc,* rep 7 times more. Join with a sl st. Fasten off.

ASSEMBLING THE TORTOISE

Work in yarn ends on all pieces. Stuff the main body, wrapping the bell rattle inside the stuffing as you do. Pin the base in place over the stuffing. Sew all around the edge firmly. Take a foot and run the yarn through

each stitch all around the last row of tr. Draw up to form a ball, and add a little stuffing to pad out. Secure and sew to one corner on the base. Do the same with the other three feet, try to keep them level so Tilly will stand flat. Take the tail and add a little stuffing, sew to the back of the shell where you joined the rounds. Take the head and stuff, shaping as you do and fatten out slightly. Sew to the front of the shell above the rim. Embroider the eyes with black. Sew the flowers at random over the shell.

Daisy the Baby Dinosaur

Every little one loves a cuddly dino to take around with them. This one is very simple and quick to make. Use bright or pastel colours. Let your imagination run wild and create a special toy for a favourite little person.

** Intermediate

YOU WILL NEED
1 x 50 g (2 oz) ball Patons Fairytale
  Dreamtime DK yarn in strawberry,
  shade 04953 (S)
1 x 50 g (2 oz) ball Patons Fairytale
  Dreamtime DK yarn in aqua, shade
  04957 (A)
Oddments of pale blue, white and green, for
  the embroidery
Black yarn, for the features
3.75 mm (UK 9, US 5) knitting needles
Safety toy stuffing
Wool needle, for sewing up
Sewing kit

SIZE
Length 30 cm (12 in) from tip of tail to nose.

TENSION
22 sts x 30 rows st st = 10 cm (4in)

DINOSAUR
BODY
Using yarn S, cast on 15 sts.
Row 1: Purl.
Row 2: Inc knitwise in each st to end (30 sts).
Now work in st st for 5 rows.
Row 8–13: Cont in st st and inc 1 st at each
end of next 6 rows (42 sts).
Row 14: (K2tog 6 times), K18, (K2tog 6 times)
(30 sts).
Work 5 rows in st st.
Row 20: K8, inc in every st to last 8 sts, K8
(44 sts).
Work 17 rows st st.

Row 38: (K2, K2tog) to end of row (33 sts).
Work 9 rows st st.
Row 48: (K1, K2tog) to end of row (22 sts).
Work 9 rows st st.
Row 58: K2tog across row (11 sts).
Work 11 rows st st.
Row 70: K2tog across row to last st, K1
(6 sts).
Break yarn and thread through rem sts, pull
up tight and fasten off. This is the tail end.

Collar
Using yarn A, cast on 30 sts.
Purl 1 row.
Row 2: K1, inc in each st to last st, K1.
Work 9 rows st st.
Row 12: Using S, K1, *yfwd, sl1, K1, psso*, rep
from * to * to last st, K1.
Row 13: Purl. Break off S and continue in A.
Work 8 rows st st.
Row 22: K2tog across row. Cast off.

Legs
Make 4
Using yarn S, cast on 10 sts.
Row 1: Knit.
Row 2: Inc in each st to end (20 sts).
Work 5 rows st st.
Row 8 (Dec row): K5, (K2tog 5 times), K5.
Knit 9 rows. Cast off.

Horns
Make 2
Using yarn A, cast on 10 sts.
Work 8 rows st st.
Row 9: K1, K2togtbl, K4, K2tog, K1.

Row 10: Purl.
Row 11: K1, K2togtbl, K2, K2tog, K1.
Row 12: Purl.
Row 13: K1, K2togtbl, K2tog, K1.
Row 14: P2tog twice.
K2tog. Fasten off.

ASSEMBLING THE DINOSAUR
Work in all ends on all pieces. Sew seam of
main body; this will run on the underside.
Leave the nose end open, stuff a little at a
time to make a firm shape. Sew the end of
the nose together with a flat seam. Sew side
and foot seam on legs, stuff firmly. Attach
to the body making sure they are level. Fold
the collar in half and stitch the side seams.
The pink line on the collar will face the front.
Sew seams on horns and lightly stuff. Stitch
in place on the front of the head. Place the
collar around the neck and slightly sloping
forward. Stitch in place.

Using contrast yarns, embroider French
knots all over the back of the dinosaur.
Embroider the nostrils and mouth with black
yarn. Cut out felt shapes for the eyes, glue
first and then oversew in place or, if you
prefer, embroider the eyes onto the face.

Soft and Squishy Playbook

Using pretty yarns from your stash, create a soft playbook for baby. Each page has a knitted and embroidered picture, and the use of plenty of bright shades of yarn add appeal for little minds. Ensure that every design is securely stitched in place for safety reasons.

✳ Beginner

MATERIALS

1 x 50 g (2 oz) ball Sirdar Snuggly Tiny Tots DK crystal blue, shade 976
1 x 50 g (2 oz) ball Sirdar Speckle DK herbie green, shade 122
1 x 50 g (2 oz) ball Sirdar Speckle DK jollie mollie (lilac), shade 125
1 x 50 g (2 oz) ball Sirdar Speckle DK lemon, shade 252
Oddments of DK yarn in lots of colours for the appliqué and embroidery
4 mm (UK 8, US 6) knitting needles
Fabric bow, for the teddy

TENSION

Is not critical for this project.

BOOK

PAGES

Make 4, one in each of the main colours
Using colour of your choice, cast on 28 sts.
Knit 6 rows garter st (every row knit).
Change to st st with a garter st border as follows:
Row 1: Knit.
Row 2: K5, P to last 5 sts, K5.
Work another 32 rows as set.
Now work 8 rows in garter st, changing colour, if you like.
Change to st st with a garter st border (as set for rows 1 and 2) for another 34 rows.
Change to garter st and work 8 more rows.
Cast off.

Sew main part of sun to page, embroider eyes and a smiley face. Take outer edge and sew around the yellow circle. Join the two ends together.

House
Using blue, cast on 16 sts.
Cont in garter st for 24 rows. Cast off.

Roof
Using green, cast on 18 sts.
Knit 2 rows.
Dec 1 st at each end of the row on the next and foll alt rows until there are 10 sts. Cast off.
Place roof onto top edge of house and sew in place. Embroider windows and doors. Sew firmly to page.

Fish
Using orange, cast on 2 sts.
Knit 1 row.
Row 2: Inc in both sts (4 sts).
Row 3: Knit.
Row 4: Inc in first st, K to last st, inc (6 sts).
Cont as set for rows 3 and 4 until there are 10 sts.
Work 6 rows garter st.
Next row: K2tog, work to last 2 sts, K2tog.
Next row: Knit.
Rep last 2 rows until 4 sts remain.
Work 2 rows on these sts.
Next row: Inc in next st, K to last st, inc.
Repeat last row until there are 14 sts.
Knit 1 row and cast off. Thread some spare yarn onto a wool needle and pull in the

Sun
Using yellow, cast on 8 sts.
Knit 2 rows.
Inc at each end of next and following alt rows until there are 16 sts.
Knit 6 rows straight.
Dec 1 st at each end of next and following alt rows until there are 8 sts.
Knit 2 rows and cast off.

Sun's outer edge
Using a random stripe yarn, cast on 5 sts.
Rows 1 and 2: Knit.
Row 3: Cast off 3 sts. K to end.
Row 4: Knit.
Row 5: Cast on 3 sts. K to end.
Repeat last 5 rows until piece, when slightly stretched, fits all around the outside edge of the sun. Cast off.

centre of the tail slightly to give shape.
Sew the fish onto the centre of the page.
Embroider an eye.

TEDDY
Using brown, cast on 9 sts.
Row 1: Inc in first st, knit to last st, inc.
Row 2: Purl.
Rep last 2 rows until there are 15 sts.
Work 4 rows st st.
Next row: K2tog, K to last 2 sts, K2tog.
Next row: Purl.
Repeat last 2 sts until there are 7 sts, ending
with a purl st. Cast off.

MUZZLE
Using brown, cast on 3 sts.
Working in garter st throughout:
Knit 2 rows.
Row 3: Inc in each st to end (6 sts).
Row 4: Knit.
Row 5: Inc in first and last st (8 sts).
Knit 4 rows.
Row 10: K2tog at each end.
Row 11: Knit.
Row 12: K2tog at each end.
Rw: Knit.
Row: K2tog twice. Cast off.

EARS
Make 2
Using brown, cast on 4 sts.
Knit 2 rows.
Row 3: Inc in first and last sts (6 sts).
Knit 4 rows.
Row 8: K2tog at each end of row.
Row 9: Knit.
Row 10: K2tog twice.
Row 11: K2tog. Cast off.

Sew muzzle onto lower centre of face and
stuff lightly to give shape. Sew the ears on
to each side of the head, gathering at the
top a little to give shape. Embroider the
features. Firmly sew a bow to the top of
the head.
  Position the teddy on the page and stitch
in place.

Car
Body
Using your choice of colour, cast on 20 sts.
Work 10 rows st st.
Cast off 10 sts. Knit to end.
Next row: Purl.
Work 4 more rows st st.
Next row: K2tog at each end of row.
Next row: Purl.
Next row: K2tog at each end of row. Cast off.

Wheels
Make 2
Using black, cast on 4 sts.
Knit 2 rows.
Row 3: Inc at each end of row (6 sts).
Knit 4 rows.
Row 8: K2tog at each end of row.
Knit 2 rows. Cast off.

Window
Using white, cast on 8 sts.
Work in st st for 8 rows ending with a purl row. Cast off.
Sew the window and wheels onto the body of the car. Embroider the triangular corner window.
Firmly sew the car to the page.

Boat
Using dark blue, cast on 8 sts.
Working in garter st, knit 2 rows.
Inc 2 sts at each end of next and foll alt rows until there are 20 sts.
Knit 1 row and cast off.

Large sail
Using white, cast on 12 sts.
Work 4 rows st st.
Row 5: Knit to last 2 sts, K2togtbl.
Row 6: Purl.
Row 7: Knit.
Row 8: Purl.
Row 9: Knit to last 2 sts, K2togtbl.
Row 10: Purl.
Repeat last 2 rows until all sts are worked off.
Fasten off.

Small sail
Using white, cast on 10 sts.
Work 4 rows in st st.
Row 5: K2tog, knit to end.
Row 6: Purl.
Work 2 rows in st st.
Row 9: K2tog, knit to end.
Row 10: Purl.
Rep last 2 rows until all sts are worked off.
Fasten off.
Arrange the pieces of the boat on the page, pin, then stitch securely in place. Embroider the mast in brown. Embroider a stripe along the base of the boat. Using red, make a flag using a few straight stitches.

Flower
Petals
Make 5
Using pink, cast on 2 sts.
Knit 1 row.
Row 2: Inc in both sts (4 sts).
Row 3: Knit.
Row 4: Inc in first st, knit to last st, inc (8 sts).

Knit 4 rows.

Row 9: K2tog, knit to last 2 sts, k2tog.

Row 10: Knit to end.

Repeat last 2 rows until there are 4 sts.

Next row: K2tog twice.

Next row: K2tog. Fasten off.

Arrange the petals in a circle on the page, then pin and sew in place. Embroider a large French knot in the flower centre. Embroider a couple of leaves at one side of the flower.

Snail

Shell

Using random stripe yarn, cast on 56 sts.

Knit 1 row.

Row 2: *Cast off 1 st in the normal way, yarn round needle, cast that st off,* rep from * to * all across row. The piece will curl up as you work.

Body

Using orange, cast on 40 sts.

Work 10 rows in garter st. Cast off.

Coil the shell into a circle, tweaking the shape a little as you go. Stitch in place. Fold the body in half lengthways and stitch into a sausage. Form the piece into a body and head. Sew in place. Embroider eyes on top of the head.

ASSEMBLING THE BOOK

Tidy all the thread ends. Put two pages tog wrong sides facing, then using a length of bright yarn threaded through a wool needle, sew the pages tog using blanket stitch. Repeat with the other two pages.

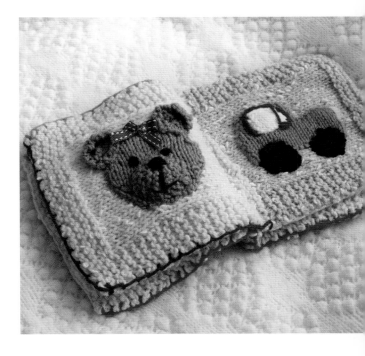

Use different colours for each side of the pages to make the book look really bright and interesting. Using a matching yarn, sew through the centre of the pages to hold them together. Make a twisted cord and thread it through the spine of the book, tie the ends in a bow. Sew the motifs onto each page, ensuring that everything is stitched very firmly. Inquisitive little hands are adept at removing bits and pieces, which could form a health and safety hazard if not properly secure. Never leave baby unattended when playing with anything attached to cords

Starry Face Ball

Even the youngest baby will enjoy holding this pretty, soft ball. With its colourful appearance and multi-coloured starry faces it is sure to please. You can also help a toddler to develop co-ordination, by teaching them to roll the ball in a specific direction and to play catch, since the ball is completely safe for indoor use.

❋ Beginner

YOU WILL NEED
Oddments of 8 different coloured DK yarns
3.75 mm (UK 9, US 4) knitting needles
Safety toy stuffing
Wool needle, for sewing up
Sewing kit

SIZE
Circumference measures 46 cm (18 in).

BALL
The ball is worked in once piece, with each of the eight sections knitted using a different colour yarn.

Using colour of your choice, cast on 34 sts.
Row 1: Knit.
**Row 2: Sl 1, knit to last st, turn.
Rows 3 and 4: Sl 1, knit to last 2 sts, turn.
Rows 5 and 6: Sl 1, knit to last 3 sts, turn.
Continue as set, working 1 less stitch at the end of every row until 8 sts remain unworked at each end.
Next row: Sl 1, knit to last 9 sts, turn.
Next 2 rows: Sl 1, knit across all stitches firmly.**
Break yarn and join in next colour.

Row 1: Knit.

Now work from ** to **.

Cont working sections in different colours until all 8 sections are complete. Cast off.

Starry Faces

Make 6

Using colour of your choice, cast on 55 sts.

Row 1: Knit.

Row 2: K4, sl 1, K2tog, psso, *K8, sl 1, K2tog,

psso*, rep from * to * to last 4 sts, K4.

Row 3: K3, sl 1, K2tog, psso, *K6, sl 1, K2tog, psso*, rep from * to * to last 3 sts, K3.

Row 4: K2, sl 1, K2tog, psso, *K4, sl 1, K2tog, psso*, rep from * to * to last 2 sts, K2.

Row 5: K1, sl 1, K2tog, psso, *K2, sl 1, K2tog, psso*, rep from * to * to last st, K1.

Row 6: *Sl 1, K2tog, psso*, rep from * to * to end (5 sts).

Break yarn and run thread through rem sts, draw up tightly and secure. Stitch side seam of face. Using black yarn, stitch a smiley face.

ASSEMBLING THE BALL

Work in all ends. Run a gathering thread around each end of the ball and draw up tightly. Join seam neatly leaving a space to stuff. Stuff firmly and make a firm, round shape. Stitch up the remaining opening. Securely sew the stars onto the ball in random positions.

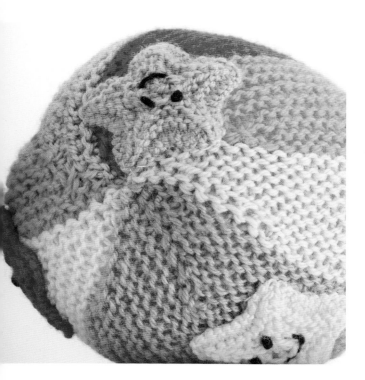

Oscar the Spotty Dog

With his cute face and eye-catching spotty markings, this little puppy is looking for a new owner. Spotty dog is quite easy to knit. Use my colour choice or create your own using remnants from your stash. Add more or less spots to his body as the whim takes you.

✳✳ Intermediate

SIZE
23 cm (9 in) sitting

TENSION
Is not critical on this project.

YOU WILL NEED
2 x 50 (2 oz) balls Sirdar Snuggly DK white, shade 257
1 x 50 (2 oz) ball Sirdar Snuggly DK baby grey, shade 427
Oddment of red DK, for the collar
4 mm (UK 8, US 6) knitting needles
3.75 mm (UK 9, US 4) knitting needles
Safety toy stuffing
Wool needle, for sewing up
Sewing kit

DOG
HEAD
Using 4 mm (UK 8, US 6) knitting needles and white, cast on 6 sts.
Row 1: Purl.
Row 2: Inc in each st (12 sts).
Row 3: Purl.
Row 4: Inc in each st (24 sts).
Row 5: Purl.
Row 6: *K1, inc in next st*, rep from * to * to end (36 sts).
Row 7: Purl.
Work 20 rows in st st, mark this line for the nose. Work another 12 rows st st.
Next row: K2tog across row.
Beg with a purl row, work 3 rows st st.
Next row: K2tog across row.

Do not cast off, run yarn through sts on needles, draw up tight and fasten off.

Body

Using 4 mm (UK 8, US 6) knitting needles and white, cast on 10 sts.
Work 2 rows st st.
Row 3: Inc in every st (20 sts).
Beg with a purl row, work 3 rows st st.
Row 7: *Inc in next st, K1*, rep from * to * to end (30 sts).
Beg with a purl row, work 5 rows st st.
Row 13: *K2, inc in next st*, rep from * to * to end (40 sts).
Beg with a purl row, work 5 rows st st.
Row 19: *K3, inc in next st*, rep from * to * to end (50 sts).
Beg with a purl row, work 7 rows st st.
Row 27: *K3, K2tog*, rep from * to * to end.
Row 28: Purl.
Work 4 rows st st.
Row 33: *K2, K2tog*, rep from * to * to end.
Row 34: Purl.
Work 8 rows st st.
Row 43: *K1, K2tog*, rep from * to * to end.
Row 44: Purl.
Work 4 rows st st.
Row 49: *K1, K2tog*, rep from * to * to last 2 sts, K2.
Row 50: Purl.
Row 51: K2tog across row. Cast off.
Fasten off. This is the neck edge.

Arms

Make 2
Using 4 mm (UK 8, US 6) knitting needles and white, cast on 14 sts.
Work 2 rows st st.
Inc 1 st at each end of the next and foll alt rows until there are 24 sts.
Work 13 rows st st.
Next row: *Inc in next st, K2*, rep from * to * to end (32 sts).
Work 9 rows st st.
Next row: *K2tog, K2*, rep from * to * to end (24 sts).
Next row: Purl.
Next row: K2tog across row (12 sts).
Next row: Purl.
Next row: K2tog across row (6 sts).
Cast off.

Leg

Make 2
Using 4 mm (UK 8, US 6) knitting needles and white, cast on 14 sts.
Work 2 rows st st.
Inc 1 st at each end of next and foll alt rows until there are 26 sts, ending on a knit row.
Work 15 rows st st.
Next row: *K2, inc in next st*, rep from * to * to last 2 sts, K2 (34 sts) (mark this line with a contrast thread to gather for paws).
Work 9 rows st st.
Next row: *K2tog, K2*, rep from * to * to end (26 sts).
Next row: Purl.
Next row: K2tog to end (13 sts).
Next row: Purl.
Next row: K1 *K2tog*, rep from * to * to end (7 sts). Cast off.

Ears

Make 2

Using 4 mm (UK 8, US 6) knitting needles and grey, cast on 9 sts.

Knit 1 row.

Working in garter st throughout, inc 1 st at each end of every row until there are 13 sts. Next work 6 rows straight in garter st.

Next row: K1, *K2tog*, rep from * to * across row. Cast off.

Nose

Using 4 mm (UK 8, US 6) knitting needles and grey, cast on 8 sts.

Work 4 rows st st.

K2tog at each end of next and foll alt rows until 2 sts remain, K2tog. Fasten off.

Tail

Using 4 mm (UK 8, US 6) knitting needles and white, cast on 12 sts.

Work 14 rows st st.

Break white yarn and join in grey yarn.

Work 2 rows st st.

Row 17: Dec 1 st at each end of next and foll alt rows until 2 sts rem, K2tog. Fasten off.

Small Spots

Make as many spots as you like

Using 3.75 mm (UK 9, US 4) knitting needles and grey, cast on 3 sts.

Row 1: Inc in first st, knit to last st, inc.

Knit 3 rows.

Row 5: Dec 1 st each end of row.

Row 6: Knit.

Row 7: Sl 1, K2tog, psso. Fasten off.

Medium Spots

Make as many spots as you like

Using 3.75 mm (UK 9, US 4) knitting needles and grey, cast on 5 sts.

Row 1: Knit.

Row 2: Inc in first and last st.

Knit 5 rows.

Next row: Dec 1 st at each end of next and foll alt row.

Next row: Knit.

Next row: Sl 1, K2tog, psso. Fasten off.

Large Spots

Make as many spots as you like

Using 3.75 mm (UK 9, US 4) knitting needles and grey, cast on 7 sts.

Row 1: Knit.

Row 2: Inc in first and last st.

Knit 7 rows.

Dec 1 st at each end of next and 2 foll alt rows.

Next row: Knit.

Next row: Sl 1, K2tog, psso. Fasten off.

Collar

Using red and 4 mm (UK 8, US 6) knitting needles, cast on 41 sts.

Row 1: K1, P1, across row to last st, K1.

Repeat last row 3 times more. Cast off.

ASSEMBLING THE DOG

Sew in all ends. The seam of the head runs along the underside. Fold the work in half and sew the seam leaving a small opening at one end to allow stuffing. Stuff quite firmly and shape as you work. Close and secure. Thread a blunt-ended needle with cream yarn and run the needle in and out of every stitch on the marked row, beg and ending at the seam. Pull the yarn quite firmly to give shape to the nose, secure the thread ends and tie off. Sew the black nose patch in place and pad out slightly. Using the picture as a guide, embroider the features. Sew French knots onto each side of the muzzle. Pin the ears in position on each side of the head and sew in place. Turn the tops of the ears forward slightly. The body seam runs up the centre back. Fold the body in half and sew seam as before, leaving an opening for stuffing. Stuff firmly and shape, then sew the opening closed. Sew the head to the body. Fold the tail in half and sew the seam, stuff lightly to give shape. Attach the tail to the back of the dog. Sew the arm and leg seams in the same way. Run a gathering thread around the base of the arms and legs at the marked rows, as for the nose, draw up firmly and secure. Attach the arms and legs to the body, remembering to place the legs so that the dog is in a sitting position and the seams are on the underside. Sew spots onto the head, body and arms in a random pattern. Sew the collar around the neck with the join at the centre back.

Hearts and Roses Mobile

No one will be able to resist this lovely crocheted nursery mobile complete with hearts and roses. I have used pinks, lemons and greens, but it would look gorgeous in any combinations of brights or pastel tones to suit a boy or a girl. I have given instructions for three basic sizes of hearts; make them in any combination you like. You could use all roses or all hearts, if you like.

❋ Beginner

YOU WILL NEED
1 x 50 g (2 oz) ball of Sirdar Snuggly DK
  spicy pink, shade 350
1 x 50 g (2 oz) ball of Sirdar Snuggly DK
  white, shade 251
1 x 50 g (2 oz) ball of Sirdar Snuggly DK
  pastel lemon, shade 320
1 x 50 g (2 oz) ball of Sirdar Snuggly DK
  summer lime, shade 260
1 x 50 g (2 oz) ball of Sirdar Snuggly DK
  pearly green, shade 304
1 x 50 g (2 oz) ball of Sirdar Snuggly DK pink
  plum, shade 443

1 x 50 g (2 oz) ball of Sirdar Snuggly DK
  petal pink, shade 215
3.75 mm (UK 9, US F 5) crochet hook
Safety toy stuffing
Plastic or wooden ring, 20 cm (8 in) in
  diameter
Craft glue
4 m (4½yd) double-sided satin ribbon in
  3 toning shades
Wool needle, for sewing up
Sewing kit

TENSION
Is not critical on this project.

Make 3 large hearts, 6 medium hearts,
3 small hearts, 6 roses and 6 leaves.

HEARTS

LARGE HEART

Make 2 for each heart and one smaller heart
to appliqué to one side of each large heart
Using your choice of colour, make 2ch, work
3dc into second ch from hook. Turn.

Next row: Work 2dc into first dc, 1dc into
next dc, 2dc into next dc (5dc).

Next row: Work 1dc into each dc to end.

Next row: Work 2dc into first dc, 1dc into
each of next 3dc, 2dc into last dc (7dc).

Next row: Work 1dc into each dc to end.
Cont to inc as before on alt rows until there
are 15 dc.
Work 2 rows without increasing.

Divide for heart

Next row: 1ch, work 1dc into each of next 7dc.
Turn.

Next row: Dc2tog, work 3dc, dc2tog. Turn.

Next row: Dc2tog, work 1dc, dc2tog. Turn.

Next row: 1dc in each dc to end. Turn.

Next row: Dc3tog. Fasten off.
Return to piece, miss centre dc, rejoin yarn to
remaining dc and work to match first side.
Place the two halves of the heart wrong
sides tog and sew around the edge, leaving
a gap for stuffing. Stuff lightly, then close up
the gap. Make a smaller heart and appliqué
it in place on front of one of the hearts.

MEDIUM HEART

Using your choice of colour, make 2ch, work
3dc into second ch from hook. Turn.

Next row: Work 2dc into first dc, 1dc into
next dc, 2dc into next dc (5dc).

Next row: Work 1dc into each dc to end.

Next row: Work 2dc into first dc, 1dc into
each of next 3dc, 2dc into last dc (7dc).

Next row: Work 1dc into each dc to end.
Cont to inc as before on alt rows until there
are 13dc.
Work 2 rows without increasing.

Divide for heart

Next row: 1ch, work 1dc into each of next
6dc. Turn.

Next row: Dc2tog, work 2dc, dc2tog. Turn.

Next row: Work in dc.

Next row: Dc2tog twice.

Next row: 1dc in each dc to end. Turn.

Next row: Dc2tog. Fasten off.
Return to piece, miss centre dc, rejoin yarn to
rem dc and work to match first side.
Place the two halves of the heart wrong
sides together and sew around the edge
leaving a gap for stuffing. Stuff lightly, then
close up the gap.

SMALL HEART

Using your choice of colour, make 2ch, work
3dc into second ch from hook. Turn.

Next row: Work 2dc into first dc, 1dc into
next dc, 2dc into next dc (5dc).

Next row: Work 1dc into each dc to end.

Next row: Work 2dc into first dc, 1dc into
each of next 3dc, 2dc into last dc (7dc).

Next row: Work 1dc into each dc to end.
Cont to inc as before on alt rows until there
are 11dc.
Work 2 rows without increasing.

Divide for heart
Next row: 1ch, work 1dc into each of next 5dc. Turn.
Next row: Dc2tog, work 1dc, dc2tog. Turn
Next row: Work in dc.
Next row: Dc2tog, work 1dc. Turn.
Next row: 1dc in each dc to end. Turn.
Next row: Dc2tog. Fasten off.
Return to piece, miss centre dc, rejoin yarn to remaining dc and work to match first side. Place the two halves of the heart wrong sides together and sew around the edge leaving a gap for stuffing. Stuff lightly, then close up the gap.

ROSES
Using your choice of colour, make 6 ch, join into a circle with a sl st.
Round 1: Work *4ch, miss 1dc, dc into next dc.* Rep from * to * five times more. Join as before.
Round 2: *Into next 4ch loop work 1dc, 3tr, 1dc*. Rep from * to * all around. Join.
Round 3: Working behind first row of petals, *insert hook from back to front and around post of dc of second row, work 1dc, 5ch.* Repeat from * to * all around. Join.
Round 4: Into 5ch loop work 1dc, 4tr, 1dc.
Round 5: Work as round 3 but with 6ch instead of 5ch.
Round 6: Work as round 5, working into 6ch loop as follows: 1dc, 1htr, 4tr, 1htr, 1dc. Join and fasten off.

LEAF
Using green, make 9ch.

Into second ch from hook, work 1dc, then 1tr into next ch, 1tr into each of next 4ch, 1htr in next ch, 1dc into last ch, do not turn but work along the other edge of the ch in the same way. Join with a sl st and fasten off. Attach a leaf to each rose.

ASSEMBLING THE MOBILE
Wind ribbon carefully around the ring, overlapping it at the start and finish to make sure it is completely covered. Glue or sew the ends together to keep in place. Cut each ribbon identically into 1 short and 1 long length. The three long lengths of ribbon will serve as the hanging ties. Stitch a rose, large heart and small heart to each of the three longer ribbons, and a heart and rose to each shorter ribbon. Thread the ribbon into a wool needle and stitch through the centres of the hearts and roses. Take a few stitches to stop each item from sliding out of place and space them apart, as desired.

Mark 6 equal points onto the ring with pins. Alternate a long and short ribbon length around the circle, pin in place to begin with. Make sure that you have sufficient ribbon pulled through on the long lengths to act as the hanging ties. Tie each length onto the ring, then take the long ends and tie them tog to form the hanging loop. You may need to adjust these lengths until you get them hanging level.

Goody Two Shoes

Create these delightful little shoes for a newborn baby in just a couple of evenings.

They are worked mostly in garter stitch so a novice knitter can attempt them. I have

used two toning yarns but you can make them in just one colour, if you prefer. Make

sure that you attach the pom poms very securely to the fronts of the shoes.

❋ Beginner

SIZE
To fit birth to 3 months

YOU WILL NEED
1 x 50 g (2 oz) ball Patons Fairytale
   Dreamtime DK, baby blue, shade 6310 (A)
1 x 50 g (2 oz) ball Patons Fairytale
   Dreamtime DK blue/pink/yellow mix, shade
   4970 (B)
3.25 mm (UK 10, US 4) knitting needles
2 small buttons
Wool needle, for sewing up
Sewing kit

SPECIAL ABBREVIATIONS
M1 = make 1 stitch as follows: pick up and knit
   the strand that lies between the stitch you
   are knitting and the next stitch, and knit
   into the back of it.

LEFT SHOE

Using yarn A, cast on 33 stitches.
Row 1: Knit.
Row 2: K1, M1, K15, M1, K1, M1, K15, M1, K1
(37 sts).
Row 3: Knit.
Row 4: K2, M1, K16, M1, K3, M1, K16, M1, K2
(41 sts).
Row 5: Knit.
Row 6: K3, M1, K14, M1, K5, M1, K14, M1, K3
(45 sts).
Row 7: Knit.
Row 8: K4, M1, K14, M1, K7, M1, K14, M1, K4
(49 sts).
*Change to yarn B and work 4 rows st st.
Row 13 (Picot row): K1, *yfwd, k2tog*, rep
from * to * to end.
Row 14: Purl.
Row 15: Knit
Row 16: Purl.*
Change to yarn A and work 14 rows garter
st. Change to yarn B.
Row 31: K16, (sl 1, K1, psso 4 times), K1, (K2tog
4 times), K16 (41 sts).
Row 32: Knit.
Row 33: K10, cast off 21 sts, knit to end. ***
Slip first set of 10 stitches on holder.
Knit 3 rows and cast off.
Rejoin yarn where you started casting off
21 sts. Cast on 13 sts.
Next row: Knit across cast-on sts and 10 sts
from holder (23 sts).
Next row (Buttonhole row): K18, K2tog, yfwd,
K1 (21 sts).
Next row: Knit. Cast off.

RIGHT SHOE

Work as for left shoe to ***. Put first set of
10 sts on holder.
Next row: K10 sts on needle; turn work and
cast on 13 sts at end of row.
Next row: Knit.
Next row (Buttonhole row): K19, yfwd, K2tog,
K1.
Next row: Knit.
Cast off all stitches on needle. Rejoin yarn to
stitches on holder.
Knit 3 rows. Cast off.

ASSEMBLING THE SHOES

Thread a wool needle with a length of
variegated yarn and a needle. With wrong
sides facing, fold the picot edge rows from
* to *, sew together matching stitch for
stitch all along the row, to form a neat picot
edging on the right side of the work. Sew
the foot and back of the shoe. Sew buttons
on to correspond with buttonholes. Using
variegated yarn make two tiny pom poms
and sew very firmly to the front of each
shoe.

Little Bunny Bag

What little girl wouldn't like to keep her special treasures in this cute little bag? It's so simple to make using stocking and garter stitches. The bunny is knitted in pieces and sewn into place on the bag. Add a sparkly butterfly motif to the bunny's hair to complete the project.

✳ Beginner

YOU WILL NEED
1 x 50 g (2 oz) ball Sirdar Snuggly Tiny Tots DK tweedy plum, shade 912
1 x 50 g (2 oz) ball Bergère de France Plume, cream (This is a fluffy yarn that knits to aran weight.)
Oddments of black and brown DK, for the embroidery
4.5 mm (UK 7, US 7) knitting needles
Butterfly motif
Small button
Safety toy stuffing
Wool needle, for sewing up
Sewing kit

TENSION
Is not crucial on this project.

SIZE
18 x 14 cm (7 x 5½ in)

BAG
Using tweedy plum, cast on 32 sts.
Work 8 rows garter st.
Change to st st and work until piece measures 28 cm (11 in).
Work 8 rows garter st. Cast off.

HANDLES
Make 2
Using tweedy plum, cast on 10 sts.
Work in garter st for 33 cm (13 in).
Cast off.

RABBIT

BODY
Make 2
Using cream, cast on 12 sts.
Work 2 rows in st st.
Inc 1 st at each end of next and foll alt row
until there are 18 sts.
Work 10 rows straight.
Dec 1 st at each end of next and foll alt rows
until 12 sts remain.
Work 2 rows st st. Cast off.

NOSE
Using cream, cast on 6 sts.
Work 2 rows st st.
Inc 1 st at each of next and foll alt rows until
there are 12 sts, ending with a purl row.
Work 4 rows st st.
Dec 1 st at each end of next and foll alt rows
until there are 6 sts.
Work 2 rows and cast off.

EARS
Make 2
Using cream, cast on 6 sts.
Work 2 rows in garter st.
Inc 1 st at each end of next and foll alt row
(10 sts).
Work 22 rows straight.
K2tog at each end of every row until 4 sts
remain. Cast off.

FRONT FEET
Make 2
Using cream, cast on 8 sts.
Work in garter st for 10 rows.

Dec 1 st at each of next and foll alt row.
Work 1 row. Cast off.

BACK FEET
Make 2
Using cream, cast on 8 sts.
Work in garter st for 8 rows.
Dec 1 st at each of next row.
Work 6 rows garter st.
K2og at each end of the next 2 rows. Cast off.

ASSEMBLING THE BAG
Fold the bag in half and mark the centre line;
this denotes back and front surfaces.

Working on the front, place a body on
the bag and stitch in place. Sew the muzzle
in the centre of the body. Before closing the
stitching, add a little stuffing to pad lightly.
Pleat the top of each ear to give shape, then
sew in place at the top centre of each side of
the body. Sew the front feet onto the base
of the body.

Embroider the eyes and nose using
contrast yarn threaded through a wool
needle then make a few straight sts on each
foot to describe the claws. Sew the butterfly
to the top centre of the bunny's head.

Sew the other body piece on the bag
back aligning it with the position of the front
body. Sew the back feet in place on each
side and embroider claws as before. Make
a small pom pom for the tail. Sew in place.
Turn right sides inside and sew the side
seams. Turn right side out. Fold each handle
in half lengthways and sew the long seam.
Sew in place on each side of the bag.

Oswald the Owl

Create your own fun patchwork owl for little ones. Worked in stocking and garter stitches, he is quite simple to knit. You will need to use separate balls of yarn for some sections and twist them together on the wrong sides of the work when changing colours to avoid holes. His eyes are felt pieces sewn onto a knitted mask. If you don't like the idea of knitting with two balls of yarn at the same time then make the owl in just one colour on each piece, he will look just as cute.

❋❋ Intermediate

SIZE
Owl stands 25 cm (10 in) tall

YOU WILL NEED
1 x 50 g (2 oz) ball of DK yarn in bright pink, turquoise, green and yellow
Oddment of cream 4-ply yarn, for the mask
Scraps of felt in pale blue, black and white, for the eyes
3.75 mm (UK 9, US 4) knitting needles
3.25 mm (UK 10, US 3) knitting needles
3.75 mm (UK 9, US F 5) crochet hook
Safety toy stuffing
Wool needle, for sewing up
Sewing kit
Glue

TENSION
Is not critical on this project.

OWL
Front Right Side
Begin at the base of the owl and using 3.75 mm (UK 9, US 4) knitting needles and pink yarn, cast on 14 sts. Work 2 rows garter st.

Change to st st and working in stripes of
2 rows turquoise and 2 rows pink , and AT
THE SAME TIME increase 1 st at the end of
the next row (this is the side edge) and at
the same edge on foll alt rows until there are
28 sts on the needle, ending on a purl row.
Break off turquoise and join in green.
Work 12 rows in stripes of 2 rows green,
2 rows pink. Break off pink.
Cont in green only for 10 rows.
Dec 1 st at the side edge of next and foll 3 alt
rows.
Purl 1 row. Cast off.

Front Left Side

Using 3.75 mm (UK 9, US 4) knitting needles
and pink yarn, cast on 7 sts, join in yellow
and cast on 7 sts. Work 2 rows garter st,
keep colours as set and twist yarns tog at
centre on the wrong side of the work to
avoid holes.
Change to st st and inc 1 st at beg of next
(this is the side edge) and every foll alt row
until there are 28 sts, ending on a purl row.
Change to blue yarn and work in st st for
another 22 rows.
Dec 1 st at side edge of next and foll 3 alt
rows. Purl 1 row and cast off.

Back Left Side

Using 3.75 mm (UK 9, US 4) knitting needles
and green yarn, cast on 14 sts.
Work 2 rows garter st. Join in yellow yarn
and change to st st, working in a stripe
sequence of 2 rows yellow and 2 rows green,
and AT THE SAME TIME inc 1 st at beg of next

(this is the side edge) and every following alt
row until there are 28 sts, ending with a purl
row.
Work another 12 rows in stripe sequence.
Join in turquoise yarn. (Twist yarns together
when changing colours to eliminate holes in
the work.)
Next row: K14 yellow, K14 turquoise.
Cont in st st for another 9 rows.
Dec 1 st at side edge of next and foll 3 alt
rows. Purl 1 row and cast off.

Back Right Side

Using 3.75 mm (UK 9, US 4) knitting needles
and green yarn, cast on 14 sts.
Work 2 rows garter st.
Change to st st and inc 1 st at the end of
next (this is the side edge) and foll alt rows
until there are 28 sts on the needle.
Work 2 more rows straight. Now join in pink
and yellow yarns.
Next row: K14 pink, K14 yellow.
Next row: P14 yellow, P14 pink.
Cont as set for another 12 rows. Break off
yellow and pink.
Join in green and work across all stitches for
another 6 rows st st.
Dec 1 st at side edge of next row and 3 foll
alt rows.
Purl 1 row. Cast off.

Feet

Make 4 in garter st
Using 3.75 mm (UK 9, US 4) knitting needles
and turquoise, cast on 20 sts.
Knit 4 rows.

Dec 1 st at each end of next and foll alt rows
until 4 sts remain.
Knit 2 rows. Cast off.

Wings
Make 4
Using 3.75 mm (UK 9, US 4) knitting needles
and pink, cast on 22 sts and work as for feet.

Eye Mask
Using 3.25 mm (UK 10, US 3) knitting
needles and cream 4-ply yarn, cast on 10 sts.
Work in garter st throughout.
***Knit 2 rows.
Inc 1 st at each end of next and foll alt rows
until there are 22 sts on the needle.
Work 8 rows straight on these stitches.
Dec 1 st at each end of next and foll alt rows
until there are 10 sts.***
Work 4 rows garter st on these stitches.
Work from *** to ***. Cast off.

Beak
Using 3.75 mm (UK 9, US 4) knitting needles
and yellow, cast on 3 sts.
Work 1 row garter st.
Row 2: Inc in first and last st.
Row 3: Knit.
Rep last 2 rows once more (7 sts).
Knit 2 rows straight.
Dec 1 st at each end of every alt row until
3 sts remain. K3tog. Fasten off.

Ear tufts
Make 2 in each of the four colours
Using 3.75 mm (UK 9, US F 5) crochet hook

make 25 ch, fasten off.

ASSEMBLING THE OWL
Work in all ends on all pieces. With right
sides facing, sew the fronts together at the
centre seam with the shaped sides on the
outside. Do the same for the back pieces.
Now place back and front together, right
sides inside and sew up base and side
seams. Stuff from the top, not too firmly,
shaping the owl as you work. Sew the top
seam together neatly.

Fold the wings in half and stitch the side
seams. Stuff lightly, sew the base. Run a
thread through from the base to the centre
of the wing, pull up and secure to give shape.
Sew wings onto each side of the owl.

Make the feet in the same way, but run
threads through at thirds to shape the toes.
Sew to the base of the owl.

Pin the eye mask in place on the centre
front of the owl, stretch a little when sewing
in place to make the mask rounded. For the
eyes, cut circles of felt in blue and black. Cut
a small V shape out of the black circle on
one side. Place the black circle onto the blue
circle, then place the eyes on the mask. Glue
and sew firmly in place. Cut a tiny circle of
white felt and add to each eye, sew in place.

Sew the beak between the eyes at the
base of the eye mask, stuff lightly.

Fold the ear tufts in half and secure.
Taking one of each colour, sew in bunches on
each side of the owl at the top of his head.

Octavia Octopus

Plain and eyelash yarns are used to create different textures in this friendly octopus. I have chosen a mix of pale pink and purple, though the toy would be equally as pretty in stripes or bright colours; you could even make each tentacle in a different colour – a perfect way to use up your stash.

❋❋ Intermediate

YOU WILL NEED
2 x 50 g (2 oz) balls Sirdar Snuggly Pearls DK pearly lilac, shade 430
2 x 50 g (2 oz) balls Sirdar Funky Fur Eyelash DK angel pink, shade 533
Small amount of Sirdar Snuggly DK spicy pink, shade 350
Oddments of black yarn, for the features
4 mm (UK 8, US 6) knitting needles
Safety toy stuffing
Wool needle, for sewing up
Sewing kit

SIZE
23 cm (9 in) from base to top of head.

TENSION
Is not critical on this project.

OCTOPUS
Body
Using lilac, cast on 84 sts.
Work 2 rows in garter st.
Change to st st and work 34 rows ending on a purl row.

Shape top
Row 1: K3, *K2tog, K4*, rep from * to * ending last rep, K2tog, K1.
Row 2: Purl.
Row 3: K2, *K2tog, K3*, rep from * to * ending last rep, K2tog, K1.
Row 4: Purl.

Working in garter st throughout, knit 2 rows.
Inc 1 st at each end of next and every foll alt
row until there are 24 sts.
Work 14 rows straight in garter st.
Dec 1 st at each end of next and foll alt rows
until there are 14 sts.
Work 2 rows. Cast off.

UPPERSIDE OF THE TENTACLES
Make 8
Using lilac, cast on 10 sts.
Row 1: K4, P2, K4.
Row 2: Knit.
The 2 rows form the pattern.
Work as set for another 44 rows.
Dec at each end of every following row until
4 sts remain by knitting 2 sts tog. Cast off.

UNDERSIDE OF THE TENTACLES
Make 8
Using angel pink, cast on 10 sts.
Work 46 rows in garter st.
Dec at each end of every row until 4 sts
remain, by knitting 2 sts tog. Cast off.

FRILL
Using spicy pink, cast on 160 sts.
Work 6 rows in garter stitch.
Work 8 rows in st st beg with a knit row.
Next row: K2tog all across row.
Cast off purlwise. Fasten off.

BOW
(Worked in garter st. Carry yarn not in use
up side of work.)
Using spicy pink, cast on 14 sts.

Row 5: K1, *K2tog, K2*, rep from * to * ending
last rep, K2tog, K1.
Row 6: Purl.
Row 7: *K2tog, K1*, rep from * to * across row.
Row 8: Purl.
Row 9: K2tog across row.
Break yarn and run through remaining sts on
needle, draw up tightly and fasten off.

BASE OF BODY
Using pink eyelash yarn, cast on 14 sts.

Work 6 rows spicy pink and 4 rows in funky fur, alternating the colourways as you go.
Rep the last 10 rows twice more.
Work 12 rows spicy pink.
**Work 4 rows funky fur, then 6 rows spicy pink.
Repeat last 10 rows twice more.
Work 4 rows funky fur and 12 rows spicy pink**
Work from ** to ** once more.
Work 4 rows funky fur, 6 rows spicy pink.
Rep last 10 rows three times more. Cast off.
Work in any loose ends on the strip of knitting. Join the two short ends together. The join will be in the centre of the underside. Thread a needle with pink yarn and sew the bow together in the centre through both thicknesses. Gather up tightly as you work to form the bow shape.

ASSEMBLING THE OCTOPUS

Sew the side seam of the body (the seam runs down the centre back). Stuff quite firmly to give a nice round shape. Pin the base in place all around the body, stretching it to fit quite tightly. Add extra stuffing, if needed, before sewing closed. Manipulate into shape, flattening the base of the body as you do. Sew the tentacles together in pairs, one lilac and one pink, matching one short straight end and with the eyelash yarn on the underside. Note that the underside tentacles are slightly longer than the upperside. Curl up the ends of the tentacles making each one of them vary in length, and sewing in place as you go. Pin the tentacles evenly around the base of the body. Sew firmly in place.

Join the short ends of the skirt together. Run some spicy pink yarn all around the cast-off edge. Slip the skirt onto the octopus and gather up slightly to fit taut around the body. Stitch in place. Embroider the facial details. Sew the bow to one side of the head.

Duckling Buggy Toy

Knit this sweet little toy to keep a tiny baby amused while in a buggy. Pretty bows decorated with attractive flower buttons alternate with cute ducklings. Loops at each end can be used to string the toy across the buggy.

✳✳ Intermediate

YOU WILL NEED
1 x 50g (2 oz) ball ball Sirdar Snuggly DK lemon, shade 252
Small amounts of DK yarn in turquoise, pale blue, pale green and orange
Black DK yarn, for the eyes
4 flower buttons
3.75 mm (UK 9, US 4) knitting needles
3.25 mm (UK 10, US F 5) crochet hook
Safety toy stuffing

TENSION
Is not critical on this project.

DUCKLINGS
Make 3
Begin at base: Using lemon, cast on 8 sts.
Row 1: Purl.
Row 2: Inc in every st (16 sts).
Row 3: Purl.
Row 4: *K1, inc*, rep from * to * to end (24 sts).
Row 5: Purl.
Row 6: *K2, inc*, rep from * to * to end (32 sts).
Row 7: Purl.
Work 20 rows st st.
Row 28: *K2, k2tog*, rep from * to * across row.
Row 29: Purl.
Row 30: *K1, K2tog*, rep from * to * across

the row.

Row 31: Purl.

Row 32: K2tog across row.

Row 33: Purl.

Break yarn and thread through sts on needles. Draw up tight and fasten off.

Feet

Make 1

Using orange, cast on 4 sts.

Knit 1 row.

Row 2: Inc in first and last st.

Row 3: Knit.

Repeat last 2 rows until there are 10 sts.

Knit 4 rows. Cast off.

BEAK

Using 3.75 mm (UK 9, US 4) knitting needles and orange, cast on 1 st.

Row 1: Inc in st.

Row 2: Inc in first st, K1.

Row 3: Knit.

Row 4: Inc in first and last st (6 sts).

Row 5: K2tog at each end of row.

Row 6: Knit.

Row 7: K2tog at each end of row.

Row 8: K2tog and fasten off.

Hanging Loops

Make 2

Using 3.25 mm (UK 10, US F 5) hook and yellow, make 12ch, join into a circle with a sl st.

Work 34dc into ring, join as before, and fasten off.

Sew the seam on the body piece, noting that the seam runs down the back of the duck. Leave a gap about half way down, stuff firmly, then close up the gap. Mark 8 rows down from the start of the head shaping. Take a needle threaded with yarn and run the yarn all around the marked row, starting and ending at the back seam. Draw up firmly to make the head, rearranging the stuffing, if necessary. Secure the thread.

Using black yarn, embroider the eyes. Take the beak and fold it in half. Sew the centre fold to the head. Sew a line through the centre of the feet and gather slightly to give shape. Sew to the base of the duckling.

Bows

Make 4

Using your choice of colour, cast on 8 sts. Work in garter st for 60 rows. Cast off. Stitch the short ends together. Flatten the loop so that the join is at the centre back. Take a needle and matching yarn, and make a running st through the centre, from top to bottom. Gather up the stitches to create a bow. Secure with a few stitches. Sew a flower button to the centre of each bow.

ASSEMBLING THE TOY

Sew the bows and ducklings tog, beg with a bow and alternating the shapes. Sew a hanging loop to each end.

Petals Baby Grab Toy

This adorable baby grab toy is made using different stitches, bobbles and cables to create textures for baby's little hands to explore. On one side the little flower is fast asleep, and on the other she is wide awake and ready to play. Add a hanging loop and use the flower as a pram toy, if you like.

✸✸ Intermediate

SIZE
21 cm (8¼ in)

YOU WILL NEED
Oddments of bright colours in DK weight yarn
3.25 mm (UK 10, US 3) knitting needles
Cable needle
Safety toy stuffing
Wool needle, for sewing up
Sewing kit

SPECIAL ABBREVIATIONS
MB = make bobble: Knit 3 times into next stitch by knitting first into the front and then into the back and then into the front again. Turn, P4. Turn, K4. Turn, P4. Turn, K4. Lift second, third and fourth stitches over the first stitch, one at a time to create a bobble.
C4B = cable 4 sts to the back: slip next 2 sts onto a cable needle and leave at the back of the work, knit the next 2 sts, then knit the 2 sts from the cable needle.

FLOWER
FLOWER CENTRE
Make 2
Using choice of colour, cast on 10 sts.
Knit 2 rows garter st.
Inc 1 st at each end of next and foll alt rows until there are 24 sts.
Work 18 rows straight on these stitches continuing in garter st.

Dec 1 st at each end of next and foll alt rows until 10 sts remain.
Knit 2 rows. Cast off.

Petal 1
Make 6
Using colour of your choice, cast on 8 sts.
Knit 2 rows garter st.
Inc 1 st at each end of next and foll alt rows until there are 14 sts.
Work straight for 8 rows in garter st.
Dec 1 st at end of next and foll alt rows until there are 2 sts, K2tog. Fasten off.

Petal 2
Make 6
Using colour of choice, cast on 9 sts.
Work in moss st as follows:
Row 1: *K1, P1*, rep from * to * across row, to last st, K1.
Row 2: As row 1.
Working the inc stitches into the pattern, inc 1 st at each of next and foll alt rows until there are 15 sts.
Work 8 rows moss st.
Dec 1 st at each end of next and foll alt rows until 3 sts remain, K3tog. Fasten off.

Petal 3
Make 6
Follow instructions for Petal 1 but work in stripes of 2 rows main colour, 2 rows contrast.

Cable Ring
Using colour of your choice, cast on 14 sts.

Row 1: P2, K4, P2, K4, P2.
Row 2: K2, P4, K2, P4, K2.
Row 3: P2, C4B P2, C4B, P2.
Row 4: As row 2.
Row 5: As row 1.
Row 6: As row 2.
Rep these 6 rows until work is long enough to fit around the inner circle of the face, ending on a row 6. Cast off.

Bobble Ring
Using colour of your choice, cast on 7 sts.
Knit 4 rows in garter st.
Next row: K3, MB, K3.
Work 5 rows garter st.
Rep last 6 rows until work fits around the inner circle of the face ending on a garter st row. Cast off.

ASSEMBLING THE FLOWER
Sew the two flower centres together around the edge leaving a small opening to stuff the shape. Stuff lightly and sew the gap closed. Stitch the petals together in pairs around the sides and leaving the base open. Stuff each lightly then sew the opening closed. Arrange the petals around the flower centre, pin in position, then stitch firmly in place. Embroider a smiley face on one side of the centre and a sleepy face on the other side. Fold the cable strip in half lengthways, stitch the seam, then join the strip into a circle. Repeat with the bobble strip. Sew a cable circle to the outer edge of one flower centre and a bobble circle to the other flower centre to cover the joins of the petals.

Pete the Penguin

Make this cheerful little fellow to bring a chuckle to someone's face. With his fat tummy and cheeky face he is sure to become a firm favourite with all ages.

✳ Beginner

SIZE
From base to top of head 30 cm (12in)

YOU WILL NEED
3 x 25 g (1 oz) balls Robin DK white, shade 70
3 x 25 g (1 oz) balls Robin DK raven (black), shade 89
2 x 25 g (1 oz) balls Robin DK gold, shade 289
Safety toy stuffing
4 mm (UK 8, US 6) knitting needles

TENSION
Is not critical for this project.

PENGUIN
Body and head are knitted in one piece.

BACK
Using black, cast on 20 sts.
Work 4 rows st st.
Row 5: *K1, inc in next st* rep from * to * to end (30 sts).
Work 9 rows st st
Row 15: *K2, inc in next st*, rep from * to * to last st, K1 (40 sts).
Work 27 rows in st st.
Row 43: *K2, K2tog*, across row to last st, K1 (40 sts).
Row 44: Purl. (When knitting Front only change to black here.)
Work 2 rows st st.

Break yarn and thread through sts on needles. Draw up and fasten off.

FRONT
Work as for back, but use white to begin with and then change to black as stated in the instructions.

WINGS
Make 2
Using black, cast on 5 sts.
Row 1: Knit.
Row 2: K2, M1, K1, M1, K2 (7 sts).
Row 3: Knit.
Row 4: K3, M1, K1, M1, K3 (9 sts).
Row 5: Knit.
Cont to inc in this way on every other row adding the extra stitches on each side as set until there are 15 sts.
Work 6 rows in garter st.
Next row: K2tog at each end of row.
Next row: Knit.
Rep last 2 rows until 3 sts remain.
K3tog and fasten off.

MASK
Using white, cast on 28 sts.
Work 8 rows st st.
Row 9: K2tog at each end of row.
Row 10: Purl.
Row 11: K2tog, K9, K2tog, Turn and work first side.
Row 12: Purl.
Row 13: K2tog, K7, K2tog.
Row 14: Purl.
Row 15: K2tog, K5, K2tog.

Row 47: K2tog at each end of row (28 sts).
Row 48: Purl.
Work 2 rows st st.
Row 51: K2tog at each end of row (26 sts).
Row 52: Purl.
Row 53: *K2, K2tog*, rep from * to * to last 2 sts, K2 (20 sts).
Work 5 rows st st.
Row 59: *K2, K2tog*, rep from * to * to end (15 sts).
Row 60: Purl.
Row 61: *K2tog,* rep from * to * to last st K1 (8 sts).

Row 16: Purl. Cast off.
Return to rem sts and complete to match first side.

FEET
Make 2
Using gold, cast on 20 sts.
Knit 4 rows.
Dec 1 st at each end of next and every foll alt row until 4 sts remain.
Knit 4 rows.
Inc 1 st at each end of next and foll alt rows until there are 20 sts.
Knit 4 rows. Cast off.

BEAK
Using gold, cast on 8 sts.
Knit 2 rows.
Dec 1 st at each end of next and foll alt rows until 2 sts remain. K2tog. Fasten off.

ASSEMBLING THE PENGUIN
Sew the back and front body together, leaving the base open for stuffing. Stuff firmly and mould into a rounded rugby ball. Pin the mask in position on the front of the penguin. Sew in place, stretching a little to get the rounded shape and ensuring each side is even. Sew the beak in the centre of the mask. Embroider the eyes on each side of the beak.

Sew the wings to each side of the penguin. Fold the feet in half.

Sew the side seams, add some stuffing to give shape, sew the base. Take some matching yarn and sew through from the base to the front of the foot in three places, radiating out from a single point at the base. Pull each point slightly to cause an indentation and create toes on the feet. Sew feet to base angling them outward slightly.

Sweetheart Blanket

Keep baby 'snug as a bug in a rug' with this cute patchwork cover. I have designed it using garter stitch squares, with the addition of a relief-work heart made up of knit and purl stitches. I have chosen traditional mixtures of pinks but you can mix and match whatever colours you like best. An easy crochet edging completes the cover, if you can't crochet then just leave the blanket edge plain, it will look just as pretty.

✳✳ Intermediate

SIZE
60 cm (24 in) square

TENSION
Each square measures 15 cm (6 in)

YOU WILL NEED
1 x 100 g (3½oz) ball Aran-weight baby yarn
  in each of four toning shades (A, B, C, D)
5 mm (UK 6, US 8) knitting needles
3.75 mm (UK 9, US F 5) crochet hook
Wool needle, for sewing up
Sewing kit

BLANKET
The blanket is made in four strips, each containing 4 squares. Each strip is worked in a specific colour and pattern sequence. Working from right to left, strips appear as follows:
Strip 1: D with heart, A plain, C with heart, B plain.
Strip 2: C plain, B with heart, D plain, A with heart.
Strip 3: B with heart, C plain, A with heart, D plain.
Strip 4: A plain, D with heart, B plain, C with heart.

Plain Square

Make 2 plain squares in each of the
4 colours: 8 in total
Cast on 25 sts.
Work 44 rows in garter st. Cast off.

Heart Square

Make 2 heart squares in each of the
4 colours: 8 in total
Cast on 25 sts.
Work 10 rows garter st.
Begin heart pattern:
Row 11: Knit.
Row 12: K12, P1, K12.
Row 13: Knit.
Row 14: K10, P5, K10.
Row 15: Knit.
Row 16: K8, P9, K8.
Row 17: Knit.
Row 18: K6, P13, K6.
Row 19: Knit.
Row 20: K5, P15, K5.
Row 21: Knit.
Row 22: As row 20.
Row 23: Knit.
Row 24: As row 20.
Row 25: Knit.
Row 26: As row 20.
Row 27: Knit.
Row 28. K5, P7, K1, P7, K5.
Row 29: Knit.
Row 30: K6, P5, K3, P5, K6.
Row 31: Knit.
Row 32: K7, P3, K5, P3 K7.
Row 33: Knit.
Row 34: K8, P1, K7, P1, K8.

Rows 35–44: Knit.
Cast off.

ASSEMBLING THE BLANKET

Work in ends neatly. Sew strips together
with right sides facing, joining the garter
st row by row with a matching yarn and
blunt-ended sewing needle. Take the needle
through alternate rows of adjacent squares,
picking up the 'little bump' made by the
garter st. Draw together firmly to give an
almost invisible seam.

Edging

Starting at one corner of the rug, join yarn
C and work a row of dc all around the edge,
working between each garter st ridge on the
side of the squares and each stitch along the
cast-on and cast-off edges. Work 3dc into
each corner to keep the edge flat.

Do not turn work but join in yarn B, and
work 1dc into each dc around rug and AT
THE SAME TIME work 3dc into each corner
dc. Work 2 more rounds in A. Join D and
work 1 round in dc.

Turn, work into each dc as follows for last
row: *1tr, 1 sl st*, rep from * to * all around
rug. Join with a sl st. Do not increase in the
corners on this round. Fasten off and work in
ends.

Duck and Owl Rattles

Using oddments of DK-weight yarns from your stash, crochet these fun duck and owl rattles to keep baby amused. Bright colours add interest as does the safety rattle inside the head.

✳✳ Intermediate

SIZE
14 cm (5½in)

TENSION
Is not critical on this project.

YOU WILL NEED
For the duck: Small amounts of bright coloured DK-weight yarns in green, pink and blue
For the owl: Small amounts of bright coloured DK yarns in pale blue, blue variegated and brown
4 mm (UK 8, US G6) crochet hook
3.75 mm (UK 9, US F5) crochet hook
Safety rattle insert
Safety toy stuffing

Wool needle, for sewing up
Sewing kit

As the rattle is worked in rounds you will need to stuff the piece as you go, and insert the rattle sound before finally closing the stitching.

DUCK
Using 4 mm (UK 8, US G 6) crochet hook and colour of your choice, make 2ch, work 6dc into second ch from hook. Join with a sl st into a circle.
Round 1: 1ch, work 2dc into each dc all around, join as before (12dc).
Round 2: 1ch, *1dc in next dc, 2dc in next dc*, rep from * to * all around, join as before (18dc).

Next round: 1ch, *1dc into next 2dc, 2dc into next dc*, rep all around, join as before (32dc).

Next round: 1ch, *1dc into each dc to end, join as before.

Rep last round 9 more times. Add rattle sound at this point, pad around with stuffing as you do.

Next round: 1ch, *1dc into each of next 2dc, dc2tog*, rep from * to * all around, join as before (24dc).

Next round: As previous round.

Next round: 1ch, *1dc into next dc, dc2tog*, rep from * to * all around, join as before (18dc).

Next round: 1ch, *dc2tog*, rep all around (9dc).

Next round: 1ch, 1dc into each dc all around, join as before.

Rep last round once more. At this point add more stuffing to make sure head is firm. Break off yarn and using a needle, thread the yarn through every dc all the way around, draw up firmly and secure with a few sts.

BEAK

Using 3.75 mm (UK 9, US F 5) crochet hook and orange, make 2ch.

Work 3dc into second ch from hook, turn.

Next row: 1dc into each dc to end, turn.

Next row: 2dc in first dc, dc in next dc, 2dc in last dc, turn, 5dc.

Next row: 1ch, work 1dc into each dc to end, turn.

Rep last row twice more.

Next row: 1ch, *dc2tog, 1dc into next dc,

Round 3: 1ch, *1dc into each of next 2dc, 2dc in next dc*, rep from * to * all around, join as before (24dc).

Round 4: 1ch, *1dc into each dc all around. Join with a sl st as before.

Continuing in rounds of dc, work:
2 rounds green,
3 rounds pink,
3 rounds green,
3 rounds blue,
3 rounds green.

Break colours and join in yellow.

dc2tog, turn.
Next row: 1ch, *1dc into each dc to end, turn.
Next row: Dc3tog and fasten off.
Fold beak in half and sew to front of head.
Embroider the eyes.

Neckband

Using 4 mm (UK 8, US G 6) crochet hook
and colour of your choice, make a chain long
enough to fit around the rattle just below the
head section.
Row 1: 1dc into second ch from hook, 1dc into
each ch to end, turn.
Row 2: 1ch, 1dc into each dc to end. Fasten
off.
Put band around neck of duck and sew
together firmly at back of neck.

OWL

Using 4 mm (UK 8, US G 6) crochet hook
and blue, make 2ch. Work 6dc into second
ch from hook. Join with a sl st into a circle.
Round 1: 1ch, work 2dc into each dc all
around, join as before (12dc).
Round 2: 1ch *1dc in next dc, 2dc in next dc*,
rep from * to * all around. Join as before
(18dc).
Round 3: 1ch, *1dc into each of next 2dc, 2dc
in next dc*, rep from * to * all around, join as
before (24dc).
Round 4: 1ch, *1dc into each dc all around,
join with a sl st as before.
Cont in rounds of dc, work 6 more rounds in
blue. Break blue.
Join in variegated yarn and work 10 more

rounds. Break variegated yarn. Join in
brown.
Next round: 1ch, *1dc into next 2dc, 2dc into
next dc*, rep from * to * all around, join as
before (32dc).
Next round: 1ch, *1dc into next 3dc, 2dc into
next dc*, rep from * to * all around, join as
before (40dc).
Next round: 1ch, *1dc into each dc to end*,
join as before.
Rep last round 10 times more. Add rattle
sound at this point, pad around with stuffing
as you work.
Next round: 1ch, *1dc into each of next 3dc,
dc2tog*, rep from * to * all around. Join as
before (32dc).
Next round: 1ch, *1dc into each of next 2dc,
dc2tog*, rep from * to * all around, join as
before (24dc).
Next round: 1ch, *1dc into next dc, dc2tog*,
rep from * to * all around. Join as before
(16dc).
Next round: 1ch, *dc2tog*, rep all around
(8dc).
Next round: 1ch, 1dc into each dc all around.
Join as before.
Rep last round once more. At this point add
further stuffing to make sure head is firm.
Break yarn and using a needle, thread the yarn
through every dc all the way around, draw up
firmly and secure with a few stitches.

Outer Eyes
Make 2
**Using 3.75 mm (UK 9, US F 5) crochet hook
and cream, make 2ch, work 6dc into second

ch from hook. Join with a sl st.

Next round: 1ch, work 2dc into each dc to end, join as before.**

Next round: 1ch, *1dc into next dc, 2dc into next dc*, rep from * to * all around, join as before.

Next round: 1ch, *1dc into each of next 2dc, 2dc into next dc*, rep from * to * all around, join as before.

Next round: 1ch, *1dc into each of next 3dc, 2dc into next dc*, rep from * to * all around, join with a sl st. Fasten off.

Inner Eyes

Make 2

Using black, work as for outer eyes from ** to **.

Sew eyes to front of head, placing cream eyes on first and then adding black eyes to centre. Sew on firmly. Using white, embroider a white stitch in the centre of each black eye. Using yellow, embroider the beak.

Neckband

Using 4 mm (UK 8, US G 6) crochet hook and colour of your choice, make a chain long enough to fit around the rattle just below the point where the head section begins.

Next row: 1dc into ch from hook, 1dc into each ch to end, turn.

Next row: 1ch, 1dc into each dc to end. Fasten off.

Put band around neck of owl and sew together firmly at back of neck.

William the Baby Whale

Babies will just love William the whale with his cheeky smile. He is made in pretty shades of blue and green pure wool and is just the right size for tiny hands to hug.

Add a safety rattle for added interest, if you like.

✳ BEGINNER

SIZE
17cm (6½ in) from nose to tail

TENSION
Is not critical on this project.

YOU WILL NEED
1 x 50 g (2 oz) ball Patons Fairytale Soft DK baby blue, shade 6310 (A)
1 x 50 g (2 oz) ball Patons Fairytale Dreamtime DK blue/aqua/green, shade 4989 (B)
1 x 50 g (2 oz) ball Patons Fairytale Dreamtime DK lime, shade 4952 (C)
Oddments of black DK, for the eyes
4.5 mm (UK 7, US 7) crochet hook
Safety toy stuffing

Wool needle, for sewing up
Sewing kit

WHALE
The main part of the whale is made all in one piece. You will need to stuff the body and head as you work.
Beg at the nose:
Row 1: Using yarn A, make 2ch, work 6dc into second ch from hook, join with a sl st to form a tight circle.
Round 2: 2dc in each dc all around. Join with a sl st (12 dc).
Round 3: 1ch, *1dc into next dc, 2dc in next dc*, rep from * to * to end. Join as before (18dc).

Round 4: 1ch, *1dc into each of next 2dc, 2dc in next dc*, rep from * to * to end (24 dc).
Round 5: 1ch, *1dc into each of next 3dc, 2dc in next dc*, rep from * to * to end (30dc).
Round 6: 1ch, *1dc into each of next 4dc, 2dc in next dc*, rep from * to * to end (36dc).
Round 7: 1ch, *1dc into each of next 5dc, 2dc in next dc*, rep from * to * to end (42dc).
Round 8: 1ch, *1dc into each of next 6dc, 2dc in next st*, rep from * to * to end (48dc).
Round 9: 1ch, *1dc into each of the next 7dc, 2dc in next st*, rep from * to * to end (54dc). Change to yarn B
Rounds 10–18: Work in rounds of dc on these 54dc.
At this point you need to begin stuffing the whale, fill the cup shape that you have already made and cont adding a little more stuffing as you go. Change to yarn A.
Round 19: Work in dc, decreasing 6 sts evenly in the round. (To decrease, work 2dc tog.)
Round 20: Work in dc.
Round 21: As round 19.
Round 22: As round 20. Change to yarn B. Cont to dec as on round 19 until there are 18dc in the round.
Work 4 rounds in dc on these 18 sts.
Stuff the whale. Break yarns and join in C. Flatten end of body between your fingers, and proceed to work tail as follows on both the upper and lower part of the body:
Working through top section to begin with, work 8dc into row ends on top section. Turn.
Next row: Work 2tr into each of next 3dc, 1dc into next 2dc, 2tr into each of next 3dc.

Next row: 1tr into each of next 6tr, sl st into each of next 2dc, 1tr into each of next 6tr.
Next row: *1tr into next tr, 2tr into next tr*, 3 times, sl st into each of next 2 sts, then rep from * to * 3 more times.
Next row: 1dc into each tr, 1 sl st into each sl st. 1dc into each tr. Fasten off. Now work other side of tail in the same way.
Place two tail sections tog and work a row of dc through both pieces all along the edge. Fasten off.

Make 2
Using yarn C, make 2dc, work 6dc into second ch from hook, join with a sl st.
Row 2: 2dc in each dc all around (12dc).
Row 3: 1ch, *dc into next dc, 2dc in next dc*, rep from * to * all around, join as before (18sts).
Row 4: 1ch, *1dc into each of next 2dc, 2dc in next dc*, rep from * to * all around, join as before (24 sts).
Row 5: 1ch, *1dc in each of next 3dc, 2dc in next dc*, rep from * to * to end, join as before (30 sts). Fasten off.
Fold circle in half and working through both thicknesses of fabric work a row of dc around the edge. Fasten off and tidy the ends.
Mould the whale into a pleasing shape with your hands. Embroider the eyes with black yarn. Pull quite firmly on each side as you do as this will give shape to the head. Work in the ends on the fins, pin in place on each side, stitch in place very firmly.

Henry the Hedgehog

With his bright red striped scarf and beady eyes Henry is all set for an afternoon adventure out and about. His prickles have been replaced with a loop stitch pattern that makes him very cuddly. He's quite simple to knit though the loop stitch part of his back takes a little time and patience to create.

❋❋ Intermediate

YOU WILL NEED
1 x 50 g (2 oz) ball of Sirdar Snowflake DK beige, shade 642 (A)
1 x 50 g (2 oz) ball of Bergere de France Cosmos marron/ecru shade 29084 (B)
Oddments of DK in red, white and black
2 x 6 mm (¼ in) black safety eyes
4.5 mm (UK 7, US 7) knitting needles
3.75 mm (UK 9, US 5) knitting needles
Safety toy stuffing
Wool needle, for sewing up
Sewing kit

SPECIAL ABBREVIATIONS
LS = Loop stitch. Insert the needle as for plain and knit 1 st, keep it on the right-hand needle, but do not slip the stitch off the left-hand needle; pass the wool to the front (as for purl) and hold under thumb, then back between the needles; knit into the same stitch and slip off; pass the first stitch over the second.

HEDGEHOG
BODY
Make 2
Using 4.5 mm (UK 7, US 7) knitting needles and yarn A, cast on 10 sts.
Work 2 rows st st.
Row 3: Inc 1 st each end of row.
Work 3 rows st st.
Rep last 4 rows until there are 22 sts.

Work 4 rows straight in st st.
Dec 1 st at each end of next and every foll third row until 12 sts remain.
Cast off. (This is the neck edge).

HEAD

Using 4.5 mm (UK 7, US 7) knitting needles and yarn A, cast on 12 sts.
Work 2 rows st st.
Row 3: Knit, increasing in every stitch to end of row (24 sts).
Row 4: Purl.
Row 5: K1, *inc in next st, K1*, rep from * to * to end of row (36 sts).
Beg with a purl row, work 3 rows st st.
Row 9: K1, *inc in next st, K2*, rep from * to * to last 2 sts, inc in next st, K1.
Beg with a purl row, work 7 rows in st st.
Shape face and nose:
Row 17: *K2, K2tog, K2*, rep from * to * to end of row (40 sts).
Beg with a purl row, work 3 rows st st.
Row 21: *K2, K2tog, K1*, rep from * to * to end of row (32 sts).
Beg with a purl row, work 3 rows st st.
Row 25: *K1, K2tog, K1*, rep from * to * to end of row (24 sts).
Row 26: Purl.
Row 27: *K1, K2tog* to end of row (16 sts).
Row 28: Purl.
Row 29: K2tog all across row (8 sts). Break off beige.
Change to black DK and work 6 rows st st.
Run yarn through the 8 sts and draw up tightly. Fasten off.

PRICKLES

Work 2-row pattern as follows:
Row 1: K1, loop st (LS) to last st, K1.
Row 2: Purl.

Using 4.5 mm (UK 7, US 7) knitting needles and yarn B, cast on 3 sts. (This end of work will be stitched centrally onto the head just above the eyes, refer to photograph for guidance.)
Knit 2 rows st st.
Row 3: Inc in first st, LS 1, inc in last st.
Row 4: Purl.
Row 5: Inc in first st, LS 3, inc in last st.
Row 6: Purl.
Row 7: Inc in first st, LS 5 , inc in last st.
Row 8: Purl (9 sts).
Row 9: Cast on 3 sts, LS to last st, K1.
Row 10: Cast on 3 sts, purl to end.
Row 11: Cast on 4 sts, LS to last st, K1.
Row 12: Cast on 4 sts, purl to end.
Row 13: Cast on 4 sts, LS to last st, K1.
Row 14: Cast on 4 sts, purl to end (27 sts).
Keeping the loop st patt correct, inc 1 st at each end on next and foll alt rows until there are 33 sts, ending on a purl row. Cont on these 33 sts working in loop pattern until there are 21 rows of loops, ending on a row 2.
Dec 1 st at each end of the next and foll alt row (29 sts).
Next row: Purl.
Keeping patt correct, cast off 4 sts at the beg of next 4 rows.
Cast off remaining 13 sts.

Ears

Make 2

Using 4.5 mm (UK 7, US 7) knitting needles and yarn A, cast on 6 sts.

Knit 4 rows.

Row 5: K2tog at each end of next row.

Row 6: K2tog at each end of next row.

Row 7: K2tog, fasten off.

Feet

Make 4

Using 4.5 mm (UK 7, US 7) knitting needles and yarn A, cast on 20 sts.

Work 10 rows st st.

Dec 1 st at each end of every alt row until 10 sts remain, end with a purl row.

Next row: K2tog all across row (5 sts).

Next row: P5tog. Fasten off.

Scarf

Carry yarn not in use neatly up the side of the work. Do not pull too tightly or work will pucker.

Using 3.75 mm (UK 9, US 4) knitting needles and white DK, cast on 8 sts.

Work in garter st stripes of 6 rows white and 6 rows red. Cont until work has 14 red stripes, end with a white stripe. Cast off.

ASSEMBLING THE HEDGEHOG

Sew in all ends neatly on all pieces. Note that the reverse st st is the right side of the work on the body, head and feet.

Turn head piece right sides inside. Sew the head seam together from the nose end, leave an opening to stuff the piece. Turn right side out. Insert the safety eyes and ensure they are firmly fixed. Stuff the head to give a round shape, and make sure the nose is firm and round. Close the opening and fasten off. Stitch a smiley mouth using black yarn.

With right sides inside, stitch body pieces together, leaving neck edge open for stuffing. Turn right sides out and stuff body, giving it a rounded shape. Close opening and secure. Stitch head onto the body, making sure its centrally positioned and very secure. With right sides inside, sew feet together, leaving base open for stuffing. Turn right sides out, stuff to give a rounded shape, stitch up base and secure. Using toning cotton and a sharp needle, form the toes. Insert the thread at the centre of a foot, pull over to opposite side of foot, thread through to the side where you began and pull firmly, this will make indentations into the piece to denote the shape of the toes. Repeat twice more, then secure the cotton firmly. Stitch the feet in position.

Work in all scarf ends. Tie the scarf around the neck, secure with a few stitches. Work in all ends of prickles piece neatly. Stitch the pointed end of the prickles onto the head just above the eyes. Position the rest of this section around the back of the head and body, stuff lightly as you go to give shape to the prickles. When you are happy with the look, stitch in place around the head and body of the hedgehog. Stitch the ears in place, one on each side of the head.

Sydney Snake

This toy can be made using oddments of yarn from your stash, I have suggested a colourscheme but you can use whatever bright shades you have to hand and change the sequence to suit your own shades.

✳✳ Intermediate

YOU WILL NEED
Oddments of Sirdar Snuggly DK in 7 bright
  colours, 25 g (1 oz) (1 ball) of each pink,
  mint, mid green, red, yellow, turquoise,
  denim blue
Oddment of black yarn, for the eyes
4 mm (UK 8, US 6) knitting needles
Safety toy stuffing
Wool needle, for sewing up
Sewing kit

SIZE
Snake measures 69 cm (27 in) from head to
tip of tail

SNAKE
Begin at head

Stripe sequence: Pink, mint, mid green, red, yellow, turquoise.

Using 4 mm (UK 8, US 6) needles and yellow, cast on 16 sts.
Row 1: Purl.
Row 2: Increase knitwise into every stitch (32 sts).
Row 3: Purl.
Row 4: *K2, inc in next st*, rep from * to * to last 2 sts, K2 (42 sts).
Beg with a purl row, work 21 rows st st.
Row 26: Purl, decreasing 6 sts evenly across the row (36 sts).
Begin body pattern:
Rows 1–2: St st in denim blue knit.

Row 3: Join in pink yarn, K1, sl 2 *K6, sl 2*, rep from * to * to last st, K1.
Row 4: Using pink, P1, sl 2, *P6, sl 2*, rep from * to * last st, P1.
Rep the last 2 rows twice more.
Rows 9-10: Knit, using denim blue.
Row 11: Join in mint, K5, sl 2, *K6, sl 2*; rep from * to * to last 5 sts, K5.
Row 12: Using mint, P5, sl 2, *P6, sl 2*, rep from * to * to last 5 sts, P5.
Rep the last 2 rows twice more.
These 16 rows form the pattern.
Cont using denim blue but alternate the colours in the sequence of pink, mint, mid green, yellow and turquoise until 13 stripes have been worked.
Keeping pattern correct, dec 1 st at each end of row on next and foll 8th rows until there are 28 sts.
Cont working in stripes of 2 rows denim blue garter st and 2 rows turquoise in st st, and AT THE SAME TIME, dec 1 st at each end of the next and foll 4th rows until 20 sts remain.
Cont in denim blue only and st st, and AT THE SAME TIME, dec 1 st at each end of the following fifth rows until there are 10 sts.
Change to red. Continuing in st st, work 18 rows, decreasing at each end as before on each foll 6th row (4 sts).
Next row: K2tog twice.
Next row: K2tog.

TONGUE
Using red, cast on 40 sts.
Knit 1 row. Cast off.

ASSEMBLING THE SNAKE
There are a lot of ends of yarns to work in so use them as best you can to stitch up each stripe on the snake. Starting at the head end, begin to sew the seam (this will run under the body and head of the snake). Stuff the head quite firmly and continue to stuff and shape as you work along the body. Add a small amount of stuffing to the tail. Shape and mould the body of the snake to get a good, even shape.

Fold the tongue in half lengthways. Push the centre of the piece inwards to form a letter 'Y' and then stitch the piece together to form the tongue. Sew firmly to the centre of the mouth. Using black yarn, embroider eyes on the snake, pulling them in quite firmly to give shape to the head.

Rosie the Rag Doll

Every little girl loves a doll to play with and Rosie will be the perfect companion, with her pretty skirt and matching top embroidered with flowers. Her hair is tied in neat braids, and she has matching pink bows.

✳✳ Intermediate

SIZE
36 cm (13¼ in) tall

TENSION
Is not critical on this project.

YOU WILL NEED
Wendy Peter Pan DK in the following shades
1 x 50 g (2 oz) ball Wendy Peter Pan DK, powder pink, shade 927
1 x 50 g (2 oz) ball Wendy Peter Pan DK white, shade 300
1 x 50 g (2 oz) ball Wendy Peter Pan DK, pistachio, bubbles shade 922
1 x 50 g (2 oz) ball Wendy Peter Pan DK, rose, shade 381

1 x 50 g (2 oz) ball Wendy Peter Pan DK milk chocolate, shade 917
Oddments of black and deep pink 4-ply yarn, for the features
Safety toy stuffing
4 mm (UK 8, US 6) knitting needles
Wool needle, for sewing up
Sewing kit

DOLL
The body and head are worked all in one piece.
Using white, cast on 36 sts.
Work 16 rows in st st.
Work 4 rows in garter st.
Change to powder pink.

Work 24 rows st st, mark this row with a loop of contrast thread for neckline.
Work 26 rows st st.
Next row: K2tog all across row.
Next row: Purl.
Next row: K2tog across row.
Next row: Purl
Break yarn and run through sts on needle, draw up tightly and fasten off.

Arms
Make 2
Using powder pink, cast on 9 sts for top of the arm.
Purl 1 row.
Row 2: Inc in each st to end of row (18 sts).
Cont in st st for another 20 rows.
Row 23: *K2, inc in next st*, rep from * to * across row (24 sts).
Row 24: Purl.
Work 6 rows st st.
Row 31: K2tog across row (12 sts).
Row 32: Purl.
Row 33: K2tog across row (6 sts).
Break yarn and run thread through sts on needle, draw up and fasten off.

Legs
Make 2
Using powder pink, cast on 20 sts.
Work 28 rows st st.
Break yarn and join in pistachio for the shoe.
Work 2 rows st st.
Row 3: K13, turn.
Row 4: P6, turn.
Row 5: K6 turn.

Rep last 2 rows twice more.
Break off yarn.
Rejoin yarn to stitches on right-hand needle and proceed as follows:
Pick up and K5 along the side of instep, 6 sts across toe, 5 sts down other side of instep, then knit across sts on left-hand needle.
Next row: Knit across all sts on needle.
Work 4 rows garter st.
Next row: K2tog, K12, K2tog, K12, K2tog.
Next row: K2tog, knit to last 2 sts, K2tog.
Next row: K9, sl 1, K2tog, psso, K9, K2tog.
Cast off.

Shoe Straps
Make 2
Using pistachio, cast on 22 sts.
Knit 1 row and cast off.

Hair Bows
Make 2
Using rose, cast on 5 sts.
Work 50 rows in garter st. Cast off.
Sew together the short ends. Fold piece in half with seam on the underside. Now take a needle and matching thread and gather the centre of the piece up firmly to make a bow. Secure with stitches.

Top
Make 2
Using rose, cast on 24 sts.
Work 4 rows garter st.
Work 28 rows st st.
Work 4 rows garter st. Cast off.

SLEEVES

Make 2

Using rose, cast on 24 sts.

Work 4 rows garter st.

Work 16 rows st st.

Work 4 rows garter st. Cast off.

SKIRT

Using pistachio, cast on 38 sts.

Work 4 rows garter st.

Work 2 rows st st.

Row 7: *K1, inc,* rep to end (76 sts).

Row 8: Purl.

Change to rose. Work 4 rows st st.

Row 13: *K3, inc*, rep from * to * to last st, K1 (95 sts).

Row 14: Purl.

Change to pistachio. Work 6 rows st st.

Change to rose. Work 4 rows st st.

Now work in garter st for the border:

Work 2 rows pistachio, 2 rows pink and 2 rows pistachio. Cast off.

ASSEMBLING THE DOLL

Sew body and head sections together, leaving base open to stuff. Seam will run down the back of the doll. Stuff the head section first, then semi-stuff the body. Take a needle and matching yarn and beg at the back seam on the marked neck row, weave the yarn in and out of every stitch, pull up tight to form the head. Cont to stuff the body section but do not close the base. Set aside.

Take the arms and sew the seam, leave the top open to stuff, then stuff quite firmly shaping the hand as you do. Leave enough fabric at the top of the arm to enable you to sew the arms to the body.

Sew through one side of the hand to form the thumb, rep on the other hand. Sew the arms to the body on each side of the shoulders. Embroider the facial features.

Starting at the foot, sew the sole and back leg seam, matching colours as you stitch. Leave the top open to stuff. Stuff the foot section first, then the rest of the leg. Fold the top of the leg flat with the seam down the centre back. Pin the legs in place inside the base of the body. Sew the body and legs together at the same time.

Sew the shoe straps in place around the ankles. Embroider a flower on the front of each shoe.

To make the hair, wind lengths of yarn around a book or stiff piece of cardboard approximately 30 cm (12 in) long. Arrange bunches of yarn across the head, sewing in place along the centre line. Cont to arrange bunches and sew them in place until the head is covered. Trim the fringe. Now divide the hair into 11 sections. Plait (braid) each section fairly loosely. Secure to the head. Divide the remaining loose ends of the plaits into two bunches. Tie each bunch tightly. Now sew the pink knitted bows securely to each bunch.

ASSEMBLING THE SKIRT AND TOP

Sew the back seam on the skirt and slip onto the doll. Secure the skirt to the waist. Sew the shoulder edges of the back and front tog.

Fold sleeve in half lengthways, mark centre point on cast-off edge. Place this point to centre join of back and front at shoulders. Sew sleeves in place onto back and fronts. Fold top in half and sew side and sleeve seams. Embroider flowers onto front of top, if desired. Slip top on to doll. It's easier to put the legs through the neck edge first and pull the top up over the doll's body. Catch the shoulders a little on each side to keep the top in place.

Freddy Fox

This little fellow is waiting for a playmate. He has a cunning smile and big bushy tail to add to his endearing character. Knitted in simple stocking stitch he can be attempted by most knitters.

❋❋ Intermediate

SIZE
30 cm (12 in) when sitting

TENSION
Is not critical on this project.

YOU WILL NEED
1 x 100 g (4 oz) ball Stylecraft Life DK copper, shade 2312
1 x 100 g (4 oz) ball Stylecraft Life DK cream, shade 2305
Oddment of black DK for the nose, ears and tail tip
Safety toy stuffing
4 mm (UK 8, US 6) knitting needles
Wool needle, for sewing up
Sewing kit

FOX
HEAD
Using copper yarn, cast on 6 sts.
Row 1: Purl.
Row 2: Inc in each st to end (12 sts).
Row 3: Purl.
Row 4: Inc in each st to end (24 sts).
Row 5: Purl.
Row 6: *K1, inc in next st*, rep from * to * to end (36 sts).
Row 7: Purl.
Work 20 rows st st (mark this final row as the nose line).
Change to cream and work another 12 rows st st.
Row 40: K2tog across row (18 sts).
Beg with a purl row, work 3 rows st st.

Row 44: K2tog across row (9 sts).
Do not cast off, run yarn through sts on needle, draw up tightly and secure.

BODY
Using copper, cast on 10 sts.
Work 2 rows st st.
Row 3: Inc in every st (20 sts).
Beg with a purl row, work 3 rows st st.
Row 7: *Inc in next st, K1*, rep from * to * to end (30 sts).
Beg with a purl row, work 5 rows st st.
Row 13: *K2, inc in next st*, rep from * to * to end (40 sts).
Beg with a purl row, work 5 rows st st.
Row 19: *K3, inc in next st*, rep from * to * to end (50 sts).
Beg with a purl row, work 7 rows st st.
Row 27: *K3, K2tog*, rep from * to * to end.
Row 28: Purl.
Work 4 rows st st.
Row 33: *K2, K2tog*, rep from * to * to end.
Row 34: Purl.
Work 8 rows st st.
Row 43: *K1, k2tog*, rep from * to * to end.
Row 44: Purl.
Work 4 rows st st.
Row 49: *K1, K2tog*, rep across row to last 2 sts, K2.
Row 50: Purl.
Row 51: K2tog across row.
Cast off.
Fasten off. This is the neck edge.

Arms

Make 2

Using copper, cast on 14 sts.

Work 2 rows st st.

Inc 1 st at each end of next and foll alt rows until there are 24 sts.

Work 13 rows st st.

Next row: *Inc in next st, K2*, rep from * to * across row (32 sts).

Work 9 rows st st.

Next row: *K2tog, K2*, rep from * to * across row (24 sts).

Next row: Purl.

Next row: K2tog all across row (12 sts).

Next row: Purl.

Next row: K2tog across row (6 sts).

Cast off.

Legs

Make 2

Using copper, cast on 14 sts.

Work 2 rows st st.

Inc 1 st at each end of next and foll alt rows until there are 26 sts, ending on a knit row.

Work 15 rows st st.

Next row: K2, *inc in next st, K2*, rep from * to * to end (34 sts). Mark last row with contrast thread as place to gather the paws.

Work 9 rows st st.

Next row: *K2tog, K2*, rep from * to * across row to last st, K1 (236 sts).

Next row: Purl.

Next row: K2tog to end (13 sts).

Next row: Purl.

Next row: K1 *K2tog*, rep from * to * across row (7 sts). Cast off.

Outer Ears

Make 2

Using black, cast on 12 sts.

Knit 4 rows st st.

Row 5: K2tog at each end of row.

Row 6: Purl.

Rep last 2 rows until 2 sts remain, K2tog and fasten off.

Inner Ears

Make 2

Work as for outer ears but use copper and cast on 10 sts instead of 12 sts.

Nose

Using black, cast on 8 sts.

Work 4 rows st st.

K2tog at each end of next and foll alt rows until 2 sts remain, K2tog. Fasten off.

Bib

Using cream, cast on 10 sts.

Purl 1 row.

Inc 1 st at each end of next and foll alt rows until there are 20 sts ending with a purl row.

Work 6 rows st st straight.

Next row: K2tog at each end of row.

Next row: Purl.

Rep last 2 rows until there are 6 sts rem. Cast off.

Tail

Using copper, cast on 12 sts.

Work 2 rows st st.

Row 3: Inc in every st (24 sts).

Beg with a purl row, work 5 rows st st.

Row 9: Inc in every st (48 sts).
Beg with a purl row, work 15 rows st st.
Row 25: K3, *K2tog*, rep from * to * to last 3 sts, K3 (39 sts).
Beg with a purl row, work 5 rows st st.
Row 31: *K2, k2tog*, rep from * to * to last 3 sts, K3 (28 sts).
Beg with a purl row, work 5 rows st st.
Break off copper and join in cream.
Row 37: *K2, K2tog*, rep from * to * across row.
Beg with a purl row, work 3 rows st st.
Break off cream and join in black.
Row 41: *K2, K2tog*, rep from * to * to end of row.
Beg with a purl row, work 3 row st st.
Row 45: K2tog across row. Run thread through rem stitches and draw up tight. Fasten off.

ASSEMBLING THE FOX

Sew in all ends. Fold the head piece in half and sew the seam leaving a small opening at one end for stuffing. The seam runs along the underside of the head. Stuff quite firmly and manipulate into shape. Stitch the opening closed. Thread a blunt-ended needle with a length of cream yarn and run it in and out of every st at the marked row, beg and ending at the seam. Pull the yarn quite firmly to give shape to the nose, secure the yarn with a few holding stitches and work in the ends. Sew the black nose in place and pad out slightly. Embroider the features. Sew pairs of black and copper ears, pin in position on each side of the head and

sew in place. Turn the tops forward slightly.

Fold the body section in half and sew the seam, leaving an opening for stuffing. Stuff firmly and manipulate into shape, then stitch the opening closed. Note the seam for the body runs up the centre back. Pin the bib in position on the body front and sew in place. Sew the head to the body.

Fold the tail in half and sew the seam. Stuff firmly and manipulate to shape. Attach the tail to the back of the fox. Sew the seams on the arms and legs in the same way, remembering they run on the underside of the pieces. Attach the arms and legs to the body, positioning the legs so that the fox is in a sitting position.

Under-the-Sea Mobile

Cheer up the nursery with this cute and colourful mobile. Baby will love to watch the little fish bobbing around. The fish are simple to knit, though assembling the mobile will take some time and patience.

✳✳ Intermediate

TENSION
Is not critical on this project.

YOU WILL NEED
Oddments of Patons Fairytale Dreamtime DK yellow, shade 4960,

Oddments of Patons Fairytale Dreamtime DK orange, shade 4951

Oddments of Patons Fairytale Dreamtime DK lime, shade 4952

Oddments of Patons Fairytale Dreamtime DK turquoise, shade 4957

Oddments of Patons Fairytale Dreamtime DK orange/green multi, shade 4971

Oddments of Patons Fairytale Dreamtime DK blue/aqua multi, shade 4989

Oddments of metallic yarns in toning shades

Black 4-ply floss, for the mouth and eyebrows

16 googly sew-on eyes

8 plastic Christmas baubles, each with an 8 in (20 cm) circumference

20 cm (8 in) embroidery hoop

2.3 m (2¼ yd) narrow satin ribbon in each of 4 toning shades

3.25 mm (UK 10, US 3) knitting needles

Craft glue

Wool needle, for sewing up

Sewing kit

MOBILE

Fish Body

Make 8, mixing and matching the colours
With choice of yarn, cast on 4 sts.
Row 1 and following alternate rows: Purl.
Row 2: Inc in each st to end of row (8 sts).
Row 4: Inc in each st to end of row (16 sts).
Row 6: *K1, inc in next st*, rep from * to * to end of row (24 sts).
Row 8: K1, *inc in next st, K2, rep from * to last 2 sts, ending inc, K1 (32 sts).
Row 10: K2, *inc, K3, rep from * to last 2 sts, ending inc, K1 (40 sts).
Work 7 rows st st beg with a purl row.
Row 18: K2, *K2tog, K3*, rep from * to * to last 3 sts, K2tog, K1.
Next and following alt rows: Purl.
Row 20: K1, *K2tog, K2*, rep from * to * to last 3 sts, K2tog, K1.
Row 22: *K1, K2tog*, rep from * to * to end.
Row 24: K2tog across row. Break yarn and run thread through sts on needle, draw up and fasten off.

Tail

Using matching yarn, cast on 5 sts.
Work 2 rows garter st and cont in garter st throughout.
Inc 1 st at each end of next and foll alt rows until there are 11 sts.
Work 8 rows straight in garter st.
Dec 1 st at each end of next and foll alt rows until there are 5 sts.
Work 2 rows garter st. Cast off.

Fins

Make 2
Using matching yarn, cast on 3 sts.
Work 10 rows st st.
Row 11: K2tog, K1.
Row 12: K2tog and fasten off.

ASSEMBLING THE FISH

Slip the body onto a bauble and sew in place. Fold the tail in half. Stitch the side seams and leave the base open. Using metallic thread, work lines of chain stitch on each side of the tail. Sew the tail firmly to the back of the fish. Sew a fin on each side of the body. Sew the eyes in place. Using black yarn, embroider a mouth and eyebrows.

Cut ribbon in varying lengths, thread a piece of ribbon through the hanging loop on top of the plastic bauble, fold over a small piece at the base and glue firmly in place.

Wind two different colours of ribbon neatly around the embroidery hoop, overlapping them as you work. Glue the ends firmly in place. Glue two equal lengths of ribbon to the top edge of the ring to form the hanging loops.

Attach the ribbons from which the fish dangle evenly around the frame. Wind the ribbon around the frame and glue in place for each of the fish.

Pumpkin

This cheery pumpkin is a perfect Halloween gift for little ones. He is lovely and soft and made in pure wool and because he is round could double up as a play ball as well as a cuddly toy. Made in garter stitch, he is simple and quick to make and only uses a small amount of yarn. You could use bright red and make him into an apple!

✱ Beginner

SIZE
46 cm (18 in) circumference

TENSION
Is not critical on this project.

YOU WILL NEED
1 x 50 g (2 oz) ball Patons Fairytale
  Dreamtime DK orange, shade 4951
Oddments of DK yarn in green, black and
  brown
Small pieces of black and white felt, for the
  eyes
Safety toy stuffing
4 mm (UK 8, US 6) knitting needles
Wool needle, for sewing up
Sewing kit

PUMPKIN
BODY
The pumpkin is worked in once piece, and is made of 8 sections.

Using orange, cast on 34 sts.
Row 1: Knit.
**Row 2: Sl 1, knit to last stitch, turn.
Rows 3 and 4: Sl 1, knit to last 2 sts, turn.
Rows 5 and 6: Sl 1, knit to last 3 sts, turn.
Cont as set, working 1 less stitch at the end of every row until 8 sts remain unworked at each end.
Next row: Sl 1, knit to last 9 sts, turn.
Next 2 rows: Sl 1, knit across all stitches firmly.**
Next row: Knit.

Next row: Purl.
Next row: K2tog all across row.
Cast off. This is the top of the hand.

FEET
Make 2
Using green, cast on 10 sts.
Work 6 rows st st.
Row 7: Inc in next st, knit to last st, inc in this stitch (12 sts).
Row 8: Purl.
Row 9: Inc in next st, knit to last st, inc in this stitch (14 sts).
Row 10: Purl.
Work 14 rows st st.
Row 25: K2tog, knit to last 2 sts, K2tog (12 sts).
Row 26: Purl.
Repeat last 2 rows once more (10 sts).
Work 6 rows in st st.
Cast off.

MOUTH
Using black, cast on 22 sts.
Knit 1 row.
Cast off.

STALK
Using brown, cast on 8 sts.
Knit 14 rows in st st.
Cast off.

LEAVES
Make 2
Using green, cast on 5 sts.
Row 1: Knit.

Now work from ** to **.
Cont working in sections until all 8 are complete.
Cast off.

ARMS
Make 2
Using green, cast on 14 sts.
Work 8 rows st st.
Row 9: *K1, inc in next st*, rep from * to * to end of row (21 sts).
Row 10: Purl.
Work 6 rows st st.
Dec 1 st at each end of next and foll alt row.

Row 2: Inc in first st, K3, inc in last st.

Row 3: K3, P1, K3.

Row 4: Inc in first st, K5, inc in last st (11 sts).

Row 5: K5, P1, K5.

Row 6: Knit.

Row 7: K5, P1, K5.

Rep rows 6 and 7 three times more.

Row 14: K2tog, knit to last 2 sts, K2tog
(9 sts).

Row 15: K4, P1, K4.

Row 16: K2tog, knit to last 2 sts, K2tog (7 sts).

Row 17: K3, P1, K3.

Row 18: K2tog, knit to last 2 sts, K2tog (5 sts).

Row 19: K2, P1, K2.

Row 20: K2tog, K1, K2tog (3 sts).

Row 21: K3.

Row 22: K3tog and fasten off.

ASSEMBLING THE PUMPKIN

Work in all ends. Run a gathering thread around each end of the body and draw up tightly. Join seam, neatly leaving an opening for stuffing. Stuff firmly to make a rounded shape, then stitch the opening closed. Thread a blunt-ended needle with orange yarn and stitch vertically along each side of every section on the body, gathering in slightly to create indentations and describe the pumpkin shape.

Fold the feet in half and sew the side seams. Stuff lightly, then sew the cast-on and cast-off ends together. Thread a needle with green yarn and working from the base of the foot, sew indentations to describe the toes by drawing the yarn through at two points along the wide edge. Sew feet to base of body, angling them outward slightly.

Sew seams on arms, stuff lightly. Sew through on one side to mark the thumb. Sew arms to sides of pumpkin.

Cut eyes from black and white felt. Arrange on the pumpkin, then glue and sew the eyes in place. Sew a smile to the face.

To make the stalk, roll the piece into a neat tube and sew down one long side. Attach to the top of the toy. Sew leaves in place beside the stalk.

Tusker the Elephant

This majestic elephant will delight children of all ages. With his brightly coloured back cloth and headdress he will cheer up any nursery. He's knitted in moss stitch, which needs to be kept correct throughout his shaping, so for that reason, he's best knitted by those with some experience.

✳✳✳ EXPERIENCED

SIZE
27 cm (11 in) tall

TENSION
Using 4.5 mm needles, 18 sts measure 10 cm (4 in) wide

YOU WILL NEED
2 x 100 g (4 oz) balls Cygnet Aran grey, shade 193
1 x 50 g (2 oz) ball of Patons Diploma Gold DK royal, shade 6170
1 x 50 g (2 oz) ball of Patons Diploma Gold DK lemon, shade 6222
1 x 50 g (2 oz) ball of Patons Diploma Gold DK red, shade 6151
1 x 50 g (2 oz) ball of Patons Diploma Gold DK apple green, shade 6125
Small scrap of white DK yarn, for the tusks
Small scrap of silver metallic yarn
Safety toy stuffing
2 black safety eyes
4.5 mm (UK 7, US 7) knitting needles
4 mm (UK 8, US 6) knitting needles
Stitch holders
Wool needle, for sewing up
Sewing kit

It is very important that you follow the pattern row by row, marking every row as you knit it. There are many increases and decreases worked and they must be made at the correct ends of the pieces.

Additionally, the moss stitch pattern has to be kept correct as you work so take care to check that you are following the continuity as you increase or decrease stitches.

The elephant is worked entirely in moss stitch unless otherwise stated. Moss stitch is created by alternating 1 knit stitch and 1 purl stitch on every row. The purl stitch is worked over the knitted stitch on the subsequent row. Work a pattern swatch first if you are not familiar with this stitch.

ELEPHANT

TRUNK
Make 2
Using 4.5 mm (UK 7, US 7) needles and grey, cast on 7 sts.
Row 1: (K1, P1) three times, K1.
Row 2: Inc in each of next 2 sts, (K1, P1) twice, K1.
Row 3: Inc in each of next 3 sts, (P1, K1) three times.
Rows 4–5: Keeping moss st correct, inc as for rows 2–3
Row 6: Inc in first st, moss st to end.
Row 7: Inc in first st, moss st to end (19 sts).
Work 2 more rows in moss st, break yarn and keep sts on a holder.

BODY AND HEAD
Make 2
Front Leg
** Using 4.5 mm (UK 7, US 7) needles and grey, cast on 13 sts.
Work in moss st for 24 rows, leave sts on a spare needle.

Back Leg
Work as for front leg for first 19 rows then proceed as follows:
Cast on 6 sts, moss st to end.
Next row: Moss st to end.
Rep last 2 rows once.
Next row: Cast on 5 sts, P1, moss st to end.
Next row: Moss st across 30 sts on needle, moss st across 13 sts of Front Leg from spare needle (43 sts).
Mark end of last row with a piece of coloured yarn to denote front of elephant.
Moss st 2 rows on these stitches.
Next row: Keeping moss st correct, inc 1 st at each end of row (45 sts).
Work 4 more rows in moss st.**
Next row: Moss st across sts of body, inc in first st of trunk, work across trunk sts, inc in last st (66 sts).
Next row: Work in moss st.
Next row: Work in moss st until 13 sts remain, cast off 5 sts, pattern to end.
Working on the last 8 sts, proceed as follows:
Next row: Work 6 rows in moss st and cast off.
Rejoin yarn to main piece of body.
Row 1: Work in moss st.
Row 2: Moss st to last 2 sts, patt 2tog.
Row 3–4: Work in moss st.
Row 5: Patt 2tog, moss st to end.
Row 6–7: As rows 3–4.
Row 8: As row 2.
Rows 9–10: as rows 3–4.
Row 11: Dec 1 st at each end of row.

Rows 12–13: As rows 3–4.

Row 14: Moss st to last 2 sts, patt 2tog.

Row 15: As row 14.

Row 16: Work in moss st.

Rows 17–18: Patt 2tog, patt to end.

Rows 19–21: Work in moss st.

Row 22: Dec 1 st at each end of row.

Rows 23–25: As rows 19–21.

Row 26: Patt 2tog, moss st to end.

Row 27: Dec 1 st at each end of row.

Rows 28–29: As rows 26–27.

Row 30: Cast off 4 sts, work to last 2 sts, patt 2tog.

Row 31: As row 26.

Row 32: Cast off 4 sts, moss st to end.

Row 33: Cast off 8 sts, moss st to end.

Row 34: Cast off 6 sts, moss st to end.

Row 35: Cast off remaining sts.

HEAD GUSSET

Using 4.5 mm (UK 7, US 7) knitting needles and grey, cast on 5 sts (this is the trunk end of the gusset).

Work 26 rows straight in moss st.

Inc 1 st at each end of next and every foll fourth row until there are 15 sts.

Work 8 rows straight.

Dec 1 st at each end of next row and then every following fourth row until there are 3 sts, K3tog. Fasten off.

SOLES OF FEET

Make 4 in garter st

Using 4.5 mm (UK 7, US 7) knitting needles, and grey cast on 5 sts.

Knit 1 row.

Inc 1 st in every alt row until there are 9 sts.

Knit 4 rows straight.

Dec 1 st at each end of every alt row until there are 5 sts.

Knit 1 row. Cast off.

UNDER BODY GUSSET

Make 2

Work from ****** to ****** on head and body piece.

Work another 2 rows in moss st. Cast off.

EARS

Make 2

Using 4.5 mm (UK 7, US 7) knitting needles and grey, cast on 5 sts.

Work 1 row moss st.

Inc 1 st at each end of next and foll alt rows until there are 13 sts.

Work another 9 rows in moss st.

Next row: Inc 1 st at each end of row.

Work 3 rows straight.

Next row: Inc 1 st at beg of row. (Mark beg of this row to denote outside edge of ear.)

Work 1 row straight.

Next row: Inc 1 st at each end of row.

Next row: Work 1 row straight (18 sts).

Work 5 rows straight in moss st.

Next row: Inc 1 st at beg of row.

Next row: Work 1 row straight.

Dec 1 st at each end of next and foll alt rows.

Cast off 2 sts at the beg of next two rows.

Cast off 3 sts at the beg of next two rows.

Cast off rem sts.

TAIL

Take 9 strands of yarn, divide into three equal pieces and make a short plait (braid) about 6 cm (2¼ in) long. Knot the ends and leave a small fringe at the end of each. Attach to back of elephant.

TUSKS

Make 2
Using 4 mm (UK 8, US 6) knitting needles and white, cast on 12 sts.
Work 4 rows st st.
Row 5: K2tog at each end of row.
Row 6: Purl.
Rep last 2 rows until 2 sts rem, K2tog, fasten off.

BACK CLOTH

Carry yarns not in use up the side of work.
Using 4 mm (UK 8, US 6) needles and red, cast on 34 sts.
Work 2 rows in garter st. Join in sliver metallic yarn.
Work 2 rows garter st. Break silver.
Using red, work 2 more rows garter st.
Join in yellow and begin patt as follows:
Rows 1–2: Using yellow, work in st st.
Rows 3–4: Using blue: K4, *sl 2, K4*, rep from* to * to end.
Rows 5–6: As rows 1–2.
Rows 7–8: Using red, K1, sl 2, *K4, sl 2* repeat from * to * to last st, K1.
Rows 9–10: As rows 1–2.
Rows 11–12: Using green, work as rows 3–4.
Rows 13–14: As rows 1–2.
Rows 15–16: Using blue, work as rows 7–8

Rows 17–18: Work as rows 1–2.
Rows 19–20: Using red, work as rows 3–4.
Rows 21–22: Work as rows 1–2.
Rows 23–24: Using green, work as rows 7–8.
Rep last 24 rows 3 times more, then rows 1–6 again.
Join in red and work 2 rows in garter st.
Join in metallic silver and work 2 rows garter st.
Join in red and work 2 rows garter st. Cast off.
Work in ends.

EDGINGS

With right side facing and using 4 mm (UK 8, US 6) needles and red, pick up and knit
64 sts evenly along one side edge of backcloth. Work 1 row garter st in red. Join in metallic silver and work 2 rows garter st, rejoin red and work 2 rows garter st. Cast off. Work other edging to match.

HEADDRESS

R = red and Y = yellow
Note You will need to use separate balls of red yarn on each side of the yellow, twisting yarns together when changing colours to avoid holes in your work.
Using 4 mm (UK 8, US 6) needles and red, cast on 25 sts.
Work 4 rows garter st.
Join in extra balls of yarn.
Row 1: K4 R, K17 Y, K4 R.
Row 2: K4 R, K2tog Y, K13 Y, K2tog Y, K4 R (23 sts).

Row 3: K4 R, K15 Y, K4 R.
Row 4: K4 R, K2tog Y, K11 Y, K2tog Y, K4 R
(21 sts).
Row 5: K4 R, K13 Y, K4 R.
Row 6–8: Work 3 more rows as set,
decreasing as before on next and foll alt row
(17 sts).
Row 9: K4 R, P9 Y, K4 R.
Row 10: K4 R, K2tog Y, K5 Y, K2tog Y, K4 R
(15 sts).
Row 11: K4 R, P7 Y, K4 R.
Cont to dec as set until 11 sts remain, ending
on a purl row.
Next row: K4 R, K3tog Y, K4 R.
Next row: K4 R, P1 Y, K4 R.
Next row: K2tog R, K2 R, K1 Y, K2 R, K2tog R
(7 sts).
Next row: K2tog R, K3 R, K2tog R.
Next row: K5 R.
Next row: Using red, K2tog, K1, K2tog.
Next row: Using red, K3tog. Fasten off.

ASSEMBLING THE ELEPHANT

Work all ends in on all pieces. With moss
st there is no right or wrong side so just
reverse the pieces when you sew them up.
Join the two underbodies neatly along the
cast-off edges.

Join the underbody to main pieces
matching legs. Join leg seams. Stitch a sole
onto the base of each leg.

Join head gusset to the two main pieces,
start at the trunk end and carefully stitch
one side at a time onto a main body and
head. Run a gathering thread around the end
of the trunk, shape and stitch up firmly. Cont
to sew up the rest of the head and body.
Mark the position of the eyes and either
insert safety eyes, or embroider the eyes,
if you prefer. Turn the seamed sides inside
and stuff the toy. Shape as you stuff. Don't
overfill the trunk; it needs to be able to curl a
little at the end.

Insert the tail and firmly sew the last part
of the body seam.

Work running st around the outside
of each ear, pull to gather very slightly to
give a rounded shape, fasten off thread
firmly. Place ears on elephant, arranging the
shaped edge onto head. Pin in place, ensure
they are level and equidistant.

Sew the side seams of the tusks and
leave the base open. Stuff firmly. Sew one
tusk to each side of the trunk.

Sew in ends on the back cloth and headdress. Using a short length of each contrast
colour make small tassels and stitch to each
corner of the back cloth and on the point of
the headdress. Sew the headdress onto the
elephant's head. Sew the back cloth to the
elephant's back around the outside edges.

Big Orange Crab

This jolly character is sure to please all babies with his bright colours and friendly smile. He is very simple to make and can be attempted by beginners. Use my colour choice or use yarns from your stash in other bright shades to give a different look.

❋ Beginner

SIZE
26 cm (10 in) from long and 15 cm (6 in) wide

TENSION
Is not critical on this project.

YOU WILL NEED
2 x 50 g (2 oz) balls of Patons Dreamtime DK orange, shade 4951
1 x 50 g (2 oz) ball of Patons Dreamtime DK orange/green/blue mix, shade 4971
1 x 50 g (2 oz) ball Patons Dreamtime DK cream, shade 4960
Small amount of black DK, for the features
Safety toy stuffing
4.5 mm (UK 7, US 7) crochet hook

CRAB
Shell is made in two pieces, upper and lower.

UPPER SHELL
******Row 1**: Using orange, make 2ch, work 6dc into second ch from hook, join with a sl st to form a tight circle.
Round 2: 2dc in each dc all around. Join with a sl st (12dc).
Round 3: 1ch, *1dc into next dc, 2dc in next dc*, rep from * to *, join as before (18dc).
Round 4: 1ch, *1dc into each of next 2dc, 2dc in next dc*, rep from * to * to end (24dc).
Round 5: 1ch, *1dc into each of next 3dc, 2dc in next dc*, rep from * to * to end (30dc).
Round 6: 1ch, *1dc into each of next 4dc, 2dc

in next dc*, rep from * to * to end (36dc).
Round 7: 1ch, *1dc into each of next 5dc, 2dc in next dc*, rep from * to * to end (42dc).
Round 8: 1ch, *1dc into each of next 6dc, 2dc in next st*, rep from * to * to end (48dc).
Round 9: 1ch, *1dc into each of the next 7dc, 2dc in next st*, rep from * to * to end (54dc).
Round 10: 1ch, *1dc into each of the next 8dc, 2dc in next st*, rep from * to * to end (60dc). Turn work.
Round 11: Work *1dc, into next dc, 1 tr into next dc*, rep from * to * all around, join as before. Fasten off. ****

LOWER SHELL

Using cream yarn, work as upper shell from **** to ****. Fasten off.

LEGS

Make 4 in orange and 2 in variegated yarn. Using 4.5 mm (UK 7, US 7) hook and your choice of yarn, make 2ch, work 8dc into second ch from hook. Join with a sl st into a tight circle.
Next round: 1dc into each dc to end (8dc). Join as before.
Cont in rounds of dc for another 18 rounds. Now add a little bit of stuffing to the leg to pad it slightly; the leg shoud bend.
Next 2 rounds: Dec 2dc on each round. Close with a sl st and fasten off.

FRONT CLAWS AND PINCHERS

Make 1 orange and 1 variegated
Using orange, make 2ch, work 12dc into second ch from hook, close with a sl st into a

tight circle.

Next round: 1ch, 1dc into each dc.

Cont working in rounds of dc on these 12dc for another 14 rounds, stuff lightly and close by dec 4dc evenly on next 2 rounds. Fasten off.

PINCHERS

Make 2 in orange and 2 in variegated yarn

Row 1: Make 2dc, work 6dc into second ch from hook. Join with a sl st.

Row 2: 1ch, *2dc in each dc*, rep from * to * all around. Join with a sl st (12dc).

Row 3: 1ch, *1dc in next dc, 2dc in next st*, rep from * to * all around. Join as before (18dc).

Row 4: 1ch, *1dc in each of next 2dc, 2dc in next st*, rep from * to * all around. Join as before (24dc).

Row 5: 1ch, *1dc in each of next 3dc, 2dc in next st*, rep from * to * all around. Join as before (30dc). Fasten off.

Fold the circle in half. Add a tiny amount of stuffing to lightly pad, and working through both thicknesses of fabric, work a row of dc around the outer edge. Fasten off and work in ends.

ASSEMBLING THE CRAB

Sew upper and lower shell together neatly, stuffing as you go to give a pleasing shape. Run a gathering thread around each leg using a blunt-ended needle and matching yarn to about half way down. Pull the thread fairly tight to shape and slightly bend the leg backwards. Repeat for all legs.

Position three legs on each side of the shell. Stitch firmly in place at the back of the shell. Stitch 2 sets of pinchers together at the base. Sew the pinchers to one end of the front claw. Shape them as you work. Make another claw and pincher to match. Curl the claws inwards to shape them. Stitch in place on each side of the shell at the front.

Rainbow Butterfly

This bright and unusual toy with its cute face and rainbow colours is sure to be adored. It could be used as a cot mobile by attaching a piece of cord firmly to the back and hanging it up to entertain a little baby.

✳✳ Intermediate

SIZE
23cm (9 in) long

TENSION
Is not critical on this project.

YOU WILL NEED
1 x 50 g (2 oz) ball Patons Fairytale Dreamtime DK orange, shade 4951

1 x 50 g (2 oz) ball Patons Fairytale Dreamtime DK green, shade 4952

1 x 50 g (2 oz) ball Patons Fairytale Dreamtime DK yellow, shade 4960

1 x 50 g (2 oz) ball Patons Diploma Gold DK violet, shade 6242

1 x 50 g (2 oz) ball Patons Diploma Gold DK red, shade 6151

1 x 50 g (2 oz) ball Patons Fairytale DK blue, shade 4957

1 x 50 g (2 oz) ball Patons Diploma Gold black, shade 6183

3.75 mm (UK 9, US 4) knitting needles

3.75 mm (UK 9, US F 5) crochet hook

Stitch holder

Safety toy stuffing

Wool needle, for sewing up

Sewing kit

BUTTERFLY
BODY AND HEAD
Using main colour choice, cast on 9 sts.
Work in st st for 2 rows.
Cont in st st, inc 1 st at each end of next row.

Row 4: Purl.

Join in contrast colour and cont in stripes of 2 rows contrast, 4 rows main, and AT THE SAME TIME inc 1 st at each end of every foll fourth row until there are 21 sts.

Next row: Purl.

Work 14 more rows in stripe pattern.

Keeping continuity of stripe pattern, dec 1 st at each end of next and every foll fourth row until 13 sts remain.

Next row: Purl. Leave this set of sts on a stitch holder or spare needle. Mark this row with a coloured thread for the end of the body section.

Now work another piece exactly the same.

Return to set of stitches left on spare needle: Using contrast colour, knit across both sets of 13 sts (26 sts).

Next row: Purl.

Next row: *K2, inc in next st*, rep from * to * to last 2 sts, K2 (34 sts).

Next row: Purl.

Work another 10 rows st st.

Dec as follows:

Next row: *K2, K2tog*, rep from * to * to last 2 sts, K2 (26 sts).

Next row: Purl.

Next row: *K2, K2tog*, rep from * to * to last 2 sts, K2 (20 sts).

Next row: Purl.

Next row: *K2, K2tog*, to end (15 sts).

Next row: Purl.

Next row: K2tog across to last st, K1 (8 sts).

Next row: Purl.

Next row: K2tog all across row (4 sts).

Next row: P4tog. Fasten off.

LARGE WINGS

Make 4 wings, 2 in each of 2 colours

Using colour of your choice, cast on 14 sts.

Work in st st for 4 rows.

Next row: Cast on 2 sts at beg of row.

Rep last row 3 more times (22 sts).

Inc 1 st at each end of every alt row until there are 28 sts.

Next row: Purl.

Cont in st st for another 12 rows ending on a purl row.

Next row: K1, sl 1, K1, psso, work to last 3 sts, K2tog, K1.

Next row: Purl.

Rep last 2 rows once.

Cast off 3 sts at beg of next 2 rows.

Cast off rem 18 sts.

SMALL WINGS

Make 4 wings, 2 in each of 2 colours

Using colour of your choice, cast on 12 sts.

Work in st st for 4 rows.

Cast on 2 sts at beg of every row, 4 times (20 sts).

Inc 1 st at each end of every alt row until there are 24 sts.

Next row: Purl.

Cont in st st for another 10 rows, ending with a purl row.

Next row: K1, sl 1, K1, psso, work to last 3 sts, K2tog, K1.

Next row: Purl.

Repeat the last two rows twice more.

Cast off 3 sts at the beg of next 2 rows.

Cast off rem 14 sts.

LEGS
Make 6
Using crochet hook, crochet a chain in black yarn approximately 12 cm (5 in) long.

FEET
Make 6, each a different colour
Using crochet hook and chosen colour, make 3ch. Now work 10tr into second chain from hook, join with a sl st to first tr. This will form a little ball, break yarn but leave a long end, thread into a large-eyed needle, then run the yarn all around the top of the ball, threading through the top of each ch, pull up tightly and secure.

FLOWERS
Using crochet hook and chosen colour, make 6ch. Join into a ring with a sl st.
Next round: Into ring work (1dc, 3ch, 6 times). Join to first dc with a sl st.
Next round: Sl st into first 3ch space, now work *1dc, 3ch, 3tr, 3ch, 1dc* into each space all around. Join with a sl st. Fasten off.

ANTENNAE
Using crochet hook and black yarn, make a chain approximately 8 cm (3½ in) long. Fasten off.

ASSEMBLING THE BUTTERFLY
Work all ends in neatly. With right sides of work facing, join side seams and head seams. Leave the cast-on end sections open to allow for turning and stuffing the piece. Use a small amount of stuffing at a time, firmly stuff the head, then the body. Stitch up the end section neatly. Thread a needle with matching yarn and run it all around the the base of the head section where it joins the body. Weave in and out of the stitches, pull the yarn tightly to form a rounded head, fasten off securely. Do the same on the body section about half way down. This will separate the body into two sections.

Take the antennae and using a crochet hook pull the piece through the top of the head from side to side. Make sure the two ends are equal, then secure them onto the head. Roll each end of the antennae into a small circle and secure.

Using black yarn, sew the eyes and a mouth onto the face.

Sew the leg pieces and thread through the upper body section as for the antennae. Space them equally on the centre body section, and ensure they are all equal in length, then secure them firmly. Stitch a foot very firmly onto the end of each leg.

Sew a pair of wings with right sides together, leaving the cast-on edges open. Turn right sides out, stuff and shape. Sew the opening closed. Do this on the other pairs of wings. Now stitch together in pairs the 2 large wings and the 2 small wings. Join the two pairs of wings together, and attach firmly to the butterfly's body at the centre back. Stitch two crochet flowers in the centre back of the wings, and one crochet flower on the top of one of the front wings.

Dog Snuggle Blanket

Make this cute little snuggle blanket, complete with a dog's head as a gift for a new baby. Crocheted in super soft yarn and a pretty lacy shell pattern it will soon become an essential part of a bedtime routine. Make sure that the dog's head is very firmly attached to the centre of the blanket for safety reasons.

❋❋ Intermediate

SIZE
30 cm (12 in) square

TENSION
Is not critical on this project.

YOU WILL NEED
2 x 50g (2 oz) balls Sirdar Snuggly DK in cream, shade 303
1 x 50g (2 oz) ball Sirdar Snuggly DK in soft brown, shade 428
Oddments of black DK, for nose and features and brown DK for the ears
4 mm (UK 8, US G 8) crochet hook

BLANKET
Using cream, make 51ch.

Row 1: 3ch, (counts as tr) miss first dc, 1tr into next dc, *1ch, miss 2dc, into next dc work (1tr, 3ch, 1tr), 1ch, miss 2dc, 1tr into each of next 3dc, rep from * ending with 1tr in each of next 2dc. Turn.

Row 2: 4ch, (counts as 1tr, 1ch), work 7tr into next 3ch loop, *1ch, miss 2tr, 1tr into next tr, 1ch, 7tr into next 3ch loop, rep from * to last 3tr, 1ch, miss 2tr, 1tr into top of turning ch. Turn (6 x shells).

Row 3: 4ch, 1tr into first tr, 1ch, miss 2tr, 1tr into each of next 3tr, *1ch, miss 2tr, into next tr work (1tr, 3ch, 1tr), 1ch, miss 2tr, 1tr into each of next 3tr. Rep from * to last 3tr, miss 2tr, into third of 4ch of previous row work 1tr,

1ch, 1tr. Turn.

Row 4: 3ch, (counts as 1tr) 3tr into first ch space, 1ch, miss 2tr, 1tr into next tr, *1ch, 7tr into next 3ch space, 1ch, miss 2tr, 1tr into next tr, rep from * to last 3tr, 1ch, miss 2tr, 3tr into last ch space, 1tr into third of 4ch at beg of previous row. Turn.

Row 5: 3ch, miss first tr, 1tr into next tr, *1ch, miss 2tr, into next tr work (1tr, 3ch, 1tr), 1ch, miss 2tr, 1tr into each of next 3tr, rep from * to end omitting 1tr at end of last rep and working last tr into third of 3ch at beg of previous row, Turn.

Rows 2–5 form patt repeat.

Work another 18 rows of pattern and fasten off.

Work edging

With right side of work facing, join cream to any corner. Work dc evenly all around the outer edge of the blanket, working into each st and row end, (approximately 50dc along each side).

Next round: 1ch, work 1dc into each dc all around outer edge, working 3dc into each corner dc, join with a sl st.

Next round: As previous round. Break cream and join in brown.

Work 1 more round of dc as before, join with a sl st. Turn work.

Next round: *1ch, 1tr in next st, sl st in next dc*, rep from * to * all around the blanket, join with a sl st. Fasten off.

DOG'S HEAD

Head is worked in rounds and you will stuff the piece as you work.

Round 1: Using 4 mm hook and soft brown make 2ch, work 6dc into second ch from hook. Join with a sl st into a circle.

Round 2: 1ch, work 2dc into each dc to end. Join with a sl st (12dc).

Round 3: 1ch, *1dc into next dc, 2dc into next dc*, rep to end. Join as before (18dc).

Round 4: 1ch, *1dc into each of next 2dc, 2dc into next dc * repeat to end. Join as before (24dc).

Work 4 rounds.

Next round: Dc in each of next 8dc, 2dc in each of next 8dc, 1dc in each of next 8dc. (32dc)

Work 5 rounds in dc.

Next round: 1ch, *1dc into each of next 2dc, dc2tog*, rep to end, join as before (24dc).

Work 2 rounds dc.

Next round: 1ch, *1dc into each of next 2dc, dc2tog*, rep to end, join as before (18dc).

Work 2 rounds dc.

Next round: 1ch, *1dc into next dc, dc2tog*, rep to end, join as before.

Work 1 round dc (12dc).

Complete stuffing head.

Next round: 1ch, *dc2tog*, rep to end, join as before (6dc).

Break yarn and run through the top of each st all around, draw up to close and fasten off.

EARS

Make 4

Using dark brown, make 4ch.

Row 1: 1dc into second ch from hook, 1dc into next 2 ch. Turn.

Row 2: 1ch, 1dc into next 3dc. Turn.

Row 3: 1ch, 2dc into first and last dc (5dc). Turn.

Row 4: 1ch, 1dc into each dc to end. Turn.

Row 5: 1ch, 2dc into first and last dc (7dc). Turn.

Work 2 rows dc.

Row 8: 1ch, dc2tog at each end of next row and foll alt rows to 3dc. Fasten off.

NOSE

Using black, make 7 ch.

Row 1: 1dc into second ch from hook, 1dc into each ch to end. Turn.

Row 2: 1ch, 1dc into each dc to end. Turn (6dc).

Row 3: 1ch, dc2tog, 1dc into each of next 2dc, dc2tog. Turn (4dc).

Row 4: Dc2tog twice (2dc).

Row 5: Dc2tog. Fasten off.

ASSEMBLING THE BLANKET

Work in the ends neatly on the blanket. Stuff the dog's head firmly. Work in any ends and close back of head. Sew ears together in pairs. Sew an ear to each side of the head. Embroider the eyes. Sew the nose in place and embroider the mouth. Fold the blanket in half and then in half again. Find the centre point and sew the dog's head very firmly to the blanket.

Monty Monkey

With his brightly coloured stripes and cheeky grin, everybody will love Monty the baby monkey. Small enough for little hands to hold, he will soon become a special playmate. Add a rattle noise to his head for added interest.

✳✳ Intermediate

SIZE
Sitting height is 30 cm (12 in)

TENSION
Is not crucial on this project.

YOU WILL NEED
1 x 50g (2 oz) ball Sirdar Snuggly DK tawny,
  shade 445 (A)
1 x 50g (2 oz) ball Sirdar Snuggly DK baby
  baby beige, shade 429 (B)
1 x 50g (2 oz) ball Sirdar Snuggly DK gold,
  shade 426 (C)
1 x 50g (2 oz) ball Sirdar Snuggly DK cream,
  shade 303 (D)

Small amount of black, for the features
Rattle insert, if desired.
3.75 mm (UK 9, US F5) crochet hook

MONKEY

Note: As the pieces to make the monkey are mostly worked in the round, stuff each part as you work.

HEAD

Worked in yarn A throughout, start at the base of the head.

Round 1: Make 2ch, work 6dc into first chain, join with a sl st to form a tight circle.

Round 2: 1ch, work 2dc into each dc to end. Join this round and all following rounds with a sl st (12dc).

Round 3: 1ch, *1dc in next dc, 2dc in next dc*, rep from * to * to end (18dc).

Round 4: 1ch, *1dc into each of next 2dc, 2dc in next dc*, rep from * to * to end (24dc).

Round 5: 1ch, *1dc into each of next 3dc, 2dc in next dc*, rep from * to * to end (30dc).

Round 5: 1ch, *1dc into each of next 4dc, 2dc in next dc*, rep from * to * to end (36dc). Work 7 more rounds without any further increase.

Add rattle insert at this point, if you like, and pad around with stuffing.

Decrease for top:

Next round: 1ch, *1dc into each of next 4dc, dc2tog*, rep from * to * to end (30dc).

Next round: 1ch, *1dc into each of next 3dc, dc2tog*, rep from * to * to end (24dc).

Next round: 1ch, *1dc into each of next 2dc, dc2tog*, rep from * to * to end (18dc).

Next round: 1ch, 1dc into each of next dc, dc2tog*, rep from * to * to end (12dc).

Next round: 1ch, dc2tog all around. Fasten off.

NOSE

Using yarn D, make 2ch.

Round 1: Work 6dc into first chain, join with a sl st to form a tight circle.

Round 2: 1ch, work 2dc into each dc to end. Join this round and all following rounds with a sl st (12dc).

Round 3: 1ch, *1dc in next dc, 2dc in next dc*, rep from * to * to end (18dc).

Round 4: 1ch, *1dc into each of next 2dc, 2dc in next dc*, rep from * to * to end (24dc). Work 4 more rounds without shaping. Fasten off.

EYE MASK

Using yarn D, make 13 ch.

Row 1: Work 1dc into second ch from hook, 1dc into each ch to end (12dc). Turn.

Row 2: 1ch, 1dc into each dc to end. Turn.

Row 3: 1ch, work 1dc into next 6dc. Turn.

Row 4: 1ch, miss first dc, 1dc into each of next 3dc, miss next dc, 1dc into last dc. Turn.

Row 5: 1ch, miss first dc, 1dc into each of next 2dc, miss next dc, 1dc into last dc. Turn.

Row 6: 1ch, dc2tog. Fasten off.

Return to remaining 6 sts and complete to match first side.

BODY

Worked in stripe sequence: 2 rows A, 2 rows B, 2 rows C

Using yarn A and starting at the base of the body:

Round 1: Make 2ch, work 6dc into first chain, join with a sl st to form a tight circle.

Round 2: 1ch, work 2dc into each dc to end,

join this round and all foll rounds with a sl st (12dc). Change to yarn B.

Round 3: 1ch, *1dc in next dc, 2dc in next dc*, rep from * to * to end (18dc).

Round 4: 1ch, *1dc into each of next 2dc, 2dc in next dc*, rep from * to * to end (24dc). Change to yarn C.

Round 5: 1ch, *1dc into each of next 3dc, 2dc in next dc*, rep from * to * to end (30dc).

Round 6: 1ch, *1dc into each of next 4dc, 2dc in next dc*, rep from * to * to end (36dc). Change to yarn A.

Round 7: 1ch, *1dc into each of next 5dc, 2dc in next dc*, rep from * to * to end (42dc). Keeping continuity of the stripe sequence throughout work another 18 rows.

Decrease for top:

Next round: 1ch, *1dc into each of next 5dc, dc2tog*, rep from * to * to end.

Next round: 1ch, *1dc into each of next 4dc, dc2tog*, rep from * to * to end.

Next round: 1ch, *1dc into each of next 3dc, dc2tog*, rep from * to * to end.

Next round: 1ch, *1dc into each of next 2dc, dc2tog*, rep from * to * to end.

Next round: 1ch, *1dc into each of next dc, dc2tog*, rep from * to * to end.

Next round: 1ch, dc2tog all around. Fasten off.

Ears

Make 2 outer ears in yarn A and 2 inner ears in yarn D.

Make 3ch. Work 12tr into third ch from hook. Turn.

Next row: 3ch, work 1tr into each tr to end.

Fasten off.

Arms and Legs

Make 4

Remember to stuff the pieces as you work. Using yarn A and starting at the top of the limb:

Round 1: Make 2ch, work 6dc into first chain, join with a sl st to form a tight circle.

Round 2: 1ch, work 2dc into each dc to end. Join this round and all foll rounds with a sl st (12dc).

Cont in rounds of dc for another 15 rounds. Complete stuffing arm or leg at this point.

Work hands or feet:

Next round: 1ch, *dc2tog* all around. Join as before (6dc). Join in yarn C.

Next round: 1ch, 2dc into each dc all around, join as before (12 dc).

Work 6 rounds in dc.

Next round: 1ch, *dc2tog*, rep from * to * all around. Fasten off.

Flatten the hand section and form into a little cup shape. Sew the top of the piece together. Thread a needle with a length of yellow yarn. Oversew with a few stitches on one side of the piece, pull in tight so it will form a thumb. Do the same on the other pieces.

Tail

Using yarn A, make 2ch.

Round 1: Work 6dc into first chain, join with a sl st to form a tight circle.

Round 2: 1ch, work 2dc into each dc to end, join this round and all following rounds with a

sl st (12dc).
Continue in rounds of dc for another 18 rounds.
Change to yarn B and work 2 rounds.
Change to yarn D and work 4 rounds.
Work 2 rounds in yarn D.
Next round: 1ch, *dc2tog all around. Fasten off.

ASSEMBLING THE MONKEY

Work in any loose ends. Form the nose into a cup shape, add some stuffing. Place on the front of the head, pin into position. Add extra stuffing, if needed, then sew in place. Centre the eye mask on the head, just above the nose. Sew in place rounding the tops of each eye piece. Embroider the features using black yarn. Sew the ears together in pairs, one A and one C. Curl them into a round shape, and sew to each side of the head. Sew the head to the body. Sew the arms and legs in place. Attach the tail to the back of the monkey.